Soldier On
Overcoming Grief by Living Through it

Enid Stronach

Cover picture – Stronach Memorial Garden at the cemetery

Library and Archives Canada Cataloguing in Publication

Stronach, Enid, 1947-
       Soldier on : overcoming grief by living through it / Enid Stronach. -- 2nd ed.

ISBN 978-1-926863-15-3

       1. Stronach, Enid, 1947-. 2. Stronach, Enid, 1947- --Family.
3. Grief. 4. Bereavement--Psychological aspects. 5. Figure skating
coaches--Ontario--Biography. I. Title.

BF575.G7S84 2011   200.92   C2010-908111-0

Library and Archives Canada registration,
book layout and/or production management
through the TRI Publishing™ division of
TRIMATRIX Management Consulting Inc.
www.trimatrixmanagement.com

Foreword

This must be what war is like. First you lose a husband, then a son, then your father-in-law. Even the family dog is taken. All in a few months, followed by deaths of mother and father. What else could happen? How do you go on? What's the point of it all?

Enid Stronach's book is an inspiring journal of one person's quest for survival, then for purpose and meaning while gradually understanding how life has changed forever. The reader might cry out: "I could never survive this; I just couldn't do it!" However, the author demonstrates the grace, the anger and the depression of grief, and thus, inspires those who face similar or lesser fates.

Enid Stronach, writing ten years later, has found a new form of life, offering considerable fulfilment and meaning. However, pain and loss are close by, now more in the background. This is a wonderful story of a woman who has been struck down with multiple losses of key loved ones in a short span of time and yet lived to speak enthusiastically of her current life. Yes, the missing persons are but a flash away from her awareness, but she can sing, dance and skate. First there is tragedy and then a miracle of recovery to a new and different life. It all happens gradually.

You will be greatly encouraged in your own hurt and sadness by Enid Stronach's writing. It took ten years before the words would flow for the author. As a pastor and family therapist, I hope that many will read this heroic story.

Soldier On my friend, Soldier On….Be brave, while yet sad.

Rev. Bill Sparling, M.Div.
Registered Marriage and Family Therapist

Acknowledgements

There are a few people that have encouraged me in writing this book. First and foremost, I thank Dennison Berwick, my editor, who made inquiries into the details of choosing a particular word, and also asked overarching questions or made suggestions that made me aware that I had not fully expressed what I intended. Without his help and knowledge, it's questionable that I would have followed through to completion. He would have preferred that I change the title from "Soldier On" to "Letter to a Widow", with the thought that I may be giving readers the idea that my topic was about war and soldiers. Although I did sometimes feel like I was experiencing the trauma of a war zone, I 'stuck to my guns' … the expression was the right fit for me. I need to express my gratitude for my friend Bill Sparling. He very kindly wrote a foreword to my book—even when I was not sure I had the workings of a book. My dear friend, Inger MacKenzie, who, upon hearing that I was writing a book, offered her home for a book signing party. I also thank Bob Aldersley for introducing me to Sheryl at Trimatrix who has been instrumental in helping me publish this book. I am very grateful for their help.

This plaque rests on a stone in
the center of our cemetery garden.

Reviews

This book by Enid Stronach is a profoundly inspiring account of triumph over unimaginable tragedy. Enid revisits her harrowing journey through loss, demonstrating how one can still say "Yes!" to life, even in the face of the multiple, unanticipated deaths of her nearest and dearest. Enid uses her life experience to help prepare us for the inevitable losses we all must face. She teaches us how to dig deep and find the courage and grace to survive, grieve and 'soldier on'.

Bonnie MacEwan-Zieman, M.Ed.
Psychotherapist

As a palliative care coordinator and nurse for many years, and also as a friend of Enid's who has followed her journey for the past 13 years, I have found Enid's resilience and courage in the face of grief to be remarkable and admirable. Her motivation to assist others in their individual grief path has led her to share her story, thereby bringing meaning to her life. We can all learn a great deal from Enid – by working through our grief, "soldiering on" and accepting what life deals us in the event of our own losses and subsequent grieving.

Andrea Hoye, RN BSN CHPCN(C)

Enid Stronach is to be admired as a truly gifted and wonderful person with so much to offer others in their time of great need, as I'm sure "Soldier On...Overcoming Grief by Living Through It" will provide. My tears were flowing with the Kleenex box next to me, and there definitely were certain parts of this book that brought back significant experiences and feelings I had when my sister died.

Mary Brown

Enid Stronach defines fortitude and grace in the face of incalculable loss – and in so doing, provides comfort and inspiration to all who know her. When from time to time we question our own actions and priorities, we need only to look at her example, and ask simply, "What would Enid do?" For this, and for her friendship, I am so very grateful.

Nancy Hudson

Engaging and thought provoking; Enid, you have amassed a great deal of insight from all your ordeals, the sound of growth evident in each line. This book should be required reading for anyone going through loss.

Tony Junor

Excerpts from notes received ...

I am in awe. Reading this book brought more depth and clarity to my understanding of the magnitude of your separate and cumulative losses, and your ability to draw on your many internal and external resources to somehow "soldier on". There are times, and you faced many, when it takes tremendous courage just to get up and go through the motions of daily life. I was impressed with your willingness to both accept and give support. I was interested in your reference to and contact with Barbara Underhill, as of course I knew of the loss of her daughter. It was so emotional and beautiful to see her honouring both her daughters as she skated in "Battle of the Blades" last winter.

Betty

I sat with tissues to hand but found it most uplifting and encouraging. Thank you. It is something that most women will have to face in the scheme of things.

Sheila

Whether it is watching Enid coaching kids on the ice, entertaining over 100 seniors at "LAFF" (Life After Fifty Five) events, singing at church, or knowing how she has 'made a difference' in my own life, it makes me want to let others share and be inspired by her strength, courage and wisdom.

Inger

I am half way through your book and have learned so much. Your writing style is excellent and makes the reader feel like we are intimately getting to know both you and your family. Thank you so much for taking the time to write such a wonderful and required book.

Laurie

With each page, I could feel your pain, despair, courage, fortitude, determination and overall strength. To have survived what life has taken from you, yet continue to forge ahead to make the best of what life has yet to offer, is remarkable. Your faith was, and is the root that keeps you seeking for the best in yourself and others. You have 'soldiered on' in the face of all adversity. Like a soldier that has seen battle, you are scarred and changed forever. Also like a soldier, you must face the future and struggle to become whole again. This fight will never end, but your growth through grief is so evident in your book. Where others might have given up, so overwhelmed with the extent of the loss, you sought to help yourself with counseling, support groups, and spiritual healing. While others may have mocked some of your means, you so correctly realized that this is your soul, your life and your need for comfort...whatever the source. SOLDIER ON my friend. You are so enriched by your experiences, knowledge and desire to help others. The world is such a better place for the likes of Enid Stronach.

Judy

"Soldier On" is a "gift" to all readers – a gift of reflection, understanding, faith and love.

Cindy

An exquisite volume; very attractive to the eye and inviting to pick up and open. This book will be a saving help to a great number of people.

Bill

I am humbled and in awe. Words seem inadequate to describe all the emotions and memories I experienced reading your book, "Soldier On". Your story, your heartfelt honesty and courage in sharing your feelings, thoughts and experiences has touched and moved my heart. From the beginning, I was compelled to read on, despite the depths of my own emotions that were surfacing. Many of us, including myself, have experienced tragedies in our lives. These losses forever change the essence of our being and our way of life. Without choice, we are propelled from life as we know it, into an entirely new and foreign direction, and all this without the love and support of our lost loved ones. It is a daunting experience. Thank you for sharing your journey. May you continue to bring comfort and hope to all who are walking the same path.

Kass

Congratulations on the interesting and motivating manner in which you sincerely and compassionately expressed your personal perspectives on grief management. The elucidations of the various social, emotional, spiritual, psychological, economic and physical challenges that are inherent in the grieving process were clearly illustrated. I do hope that those who are faced with similar experiences can use your work as a guideline for "Soldiering On."

Awadh

I believe your story will touch people who are struggling through their grief. There are so many books of this nature out there. There always will be because it just simply is...life. Your story is lovingly told, succinctly written, with honesty and from the heart. It will touch the lives of those that really need it and bring a sense of peace.

Debbie

Enid Stronach's writing is easy to read and fast paced. We live in an era in which inspiration is now considered very important by many. It may be that many people are more cynical today of leaders, sports heroes and politicians. But as in a sermon at church, many publications need to be there to inspire others to move beyond their comfort zone and get the feeling that they can live on for another day. Enid has done that, and while she is a uniquely positive person, many others will be inspired to try again to have faith in the future, thanks to her experience and her writing.

Bill

Excellent book.   It is powerful, courageous and inspirational.

Lyndsey

We devoured this wonderful book.   Reading through this honest and heartfelt writing will help many people who are broken.

Sherrie

Table of Contents

Cemetery Garden

Introduction

"Just Do It"…those were the words that came to mind after years of contemplating my long-standing desire to write a book. "About what? Where do I start?" I asked myself. I've always listened carefully to those messages that seemed to come just when I most needed direction - some so profound that they have strengthened my belief in a Higher Power. (I'll talk about these messages later on.) Three friends had written books; surely I was also capable of accomplishing this for myself?

Paper, pen, and a relaxing girls week at Laurie's cottage beside Lake Wollaston, Ontario, seemed a fitting place to begin. Nestled on a hill overlooking the beautiful scenery, Castle Blayney is our retreat where my girlfriends and I have met once a year for the past fifteen years or so. It gets its name from a community in Ireland, not a castle; but to us, it surely is. It's a place where we reconnect. For some, it's the only time we see each other during the year, yet it's as if we've never been apart. The pleasures are many: Getting in touch with nature, laughing a lot, and simply rejuvenating our souls while enjoying the peaceful and serene surroundings. Most of the girls enjoy playing cards, but for me, this has always been a time to catch up on my letter writing. Because of technology, and my introduction to computers and e-mailing, hand-written letters have almost become a pleasure of the past. However, writing is an enjoyment I still find time for.

Sitting down to write this book, I sensed I was beginning a journey that was going to demand much more of my energy, time and emotional involvement than I imagined. So it has proved to be. How could it be otherwise? The journey has not been one of miles, but an odyssey towards awareness and understanding of deeper truths in the context of my own life. I believe every one of us is embarked on such a journey, whether we are aware of it or not. Perhaps that's God's true purpose for us on this Earth.

I offer this story of my own odyssey through grief in the hope that whatever I may have learned may also help others. All of us lose people we love. All of us face a journey through grief that is daunting and, at times, overwhelming. If these words give any encouragement and support to fellow travellers, they will be worth all the effort it has taken me to write them.

My Beloved Bill

Life, as I knew it, changed completely one day in October, eleven years ago. Our evening began perfectly normally; I left my husband Bill and younger son Richard enjoying a Swiss Chalet ribs and chicken dinner together in front of the T.V. while I went to final rehearsals for Lil' Abner, in which I had a principal role. I still have their dinner receipt from that night - a small part of them I don't want to discard. They wished me fun and off I went. Our other son, Steven, was out for the evening.

Several hours later I arrived home to find the house eerily silent. There wasn't the usual cheery greeting from my husband, "Hi Luv!" as I came through the door. Though momentarily disappointed, I just assumed he was out with Kipper, our 13-year-old Labrador retriever, for their usual nightly walk.

I started to climb the stairs. As I reached the top, I saw Kipper laying at the entrance to Steven's bedroom. Bill was close-by, lying on the floor.

His arms were folded comfortably across his chest, his glasses placed neatly at his side. He'd been doing some carpentry work to a cupboard in Steve's room. I didn't like Bill's look as soon as I saw him, nor his feel when I touched him, but I couldn't comprehend the reality of what I must have recognized immediately somewhere deep inside myself. I called 911 and, following their directions and through my tears, I tried to resuscitate him. All was in vain. Then the truth and the horror of my discovery set in - my loving husband of 27 years was dead!

Paramedics and fire-fighters arrived in what seemed like no time at all. Perhaps this was the beginning of that warping of time and priorities that comes with sudden shocks and overwhelming grief. A female police officer drove me to the hospital, where my husband was pronounced dead.

I was directed into a small room to wait for my sons, Steven, aged 23, and Richard, aged 16. There was a care worker from Victim Services in the room. He didn't speak, and though I'm sure he meant well and was trained to help, his presence made me uncomfortable. I was relieved when my sons arrived soon afterwards. Richard, who'd been eating dinner with his father only three hours earlier, stood in stunned silence. His face was etched with the deep shock and pain we were all feeling at such a sudden, unexpected loss. Steven was also silent, perhaps trying to push away the shock, anger and grief that would later overwhelm him. We said very little.

It was after 11:00 p.m. and I decided it was too late to disturb family or friends to ask them to come to our aid. Informing our parents at that time of night was not to be considered, as far as I was concerned; better to allow them a good night's sleep, and to break the horrible news to them in person in the morning. My parents lived close-by; Bill's parents lived a two-hour drive away.

However, at the insistence of the fire-fighters, my friend Dave was called. He was also a fire-fighter and, apparently coincidently, on duty that night. He notified his wife Jan and other friends, so it wasn't long before my support was in place. Some girlfriends of mine had gone to Buffalo, in the U.S., for a weekend of shopping, but as soon as they heard, they returned to Canada and by the early hours of the morning were at my side. My cousin and her husband also came home from their cottage after I called them in the morning.

I don't remember how we got home from the hospital. A few hours earlier Steven, Richard and I had left a happy, boisterous family home. Now we returned to a silent house that would never again hear our beloved Bill's voice. My world, and the world of my two sons, was shattered. Where would we ever find the strength to go on, let alone rebuild our lives and to continue the life journey that had stopped so abruptly for my Bill, just three days before his 51st birthday?

Bill died of an acute heart attack, caused by coronary artery disease. There had been no history and no signs, though looking back on the months before his death I feel there might have been signs that he chose to ignore. For example, I always questioned his need for Tums. "Just a little indigestion," he'd say. Bill had a knack for downplaying any little ache or pain. He was always trying to save me concern. Our family doctor reported that the only way to have detected his problem would have been a stress test. Those were not so popular 10 years ago. Nowadays the test seems to be given routinely to determine whether an artery is blocked and, if so, it can be treated with by-pass surgery. Tragically, Bill was not one of today's lucky ones.

My life had been a comfortable one, happy and busy with the normal activities and healthy balance of work, school, sports and social gatherings. Having lived in Oakville for fourteen years, our close contact with family and friends was most positive and always fun. We had a large network of support.

I can't help but wonder if things might have been different had I been home that night. Would he be alive today if he had gotten into hospital? I will never know and I try not to carry guilt, although it is sometimes very difficult. I don't do the big shows like I used to. It's such a commitment, but perhaps I fear what I might come home to.

More than 500 guests attended Bill's funeral. I greeted and spoke to all of them. Food was abundant, prepared and served by many wonderful friends. Neither Bill nor I had siblings, but over many years we'd both built many strong friendships through Bill's work and with our neighbours, as well as my sorority, dance, skating, theatre, and the other activities we took part in, such as baseball, soccer and hockey.

In our hour of need, family and friends rallied round Steven, Richard, and me. In those early days of our new world without husband and without father, they helped to sustain us with their love and by taking care of so many details that seemed to overwhelm us. I will be forever grateful to my family and many friends; if they ever read these words they will know the extent of my appreciation for their caring and kindnesses through this journey of healing. Coming back to our home from the funeral, with my wonderful family around me, everything seemed to be surreal. We just could not believe Bill was gone. We all sat around the kitchen table, opened to its full extent, and spread with plates of food.

Without my family, although not large, I don't know where I would be today. Sharing our vulnerabilities is what creates truly close bonds in relationships, I believe. It is important to reach out to those trusted and precious people who care about us the most. Auntie Nette, my mom's sister, remains a huge support, as does Muriel, my mother-in-law. Of course, my mom and dad were there too. We were all suffering so much, but knew we would receive each other's nurturing care as we faced this difficult and painful journey ahead.

My husband's father, Bill Sr., was in failing health, on oxygen, but he came with Nana to their son's funeral, and stayed a few days with us in Oakville. In fact, it took two cars to fetch them from Belleville. Steven drove one car and a friend, Bob, brought the extra oxygen tank Bill Sr. required. How unnatural it must have been for Bill Sr. and Nana to be coming to bury their son. Shouldn't it be the other way around? Our children aren't supposed to die before us. And so I ached for them too.

Life goes on; friends cannot stay forever. After the funeral, gradually, they must return to their normal lives. Yet what was normal for us now? My poor boys...Steven, 23, and Richard, 16, had never known tragedy. Nor had I. Every day, millions of people around the world face death and overwhelming difficulties and manage to get through them. I vowed that we would too. Yet without our father and husband, we were completely disorientated; coping seemed to require a superhuman effort that on some days I was unable to summon. Many days were dark, empty, and full of tears. And I confess that there were times I thought it would be easier to join Bill than to try to carry on in this world. What a terrible thought, even to consider this! Thankfully, I was not prone to depression. Supporting my boys and getting through to the next day became my focus and my support.

The nights were so hard, and waking up, even harder, as I realized my reality. We've all heard of receiving signals and I wondered if I was getting one when the alarm in the upstairs hall went off in the middle of the night. It hadn't happened before and it hasn't happened since in 27 years, but a short while after Bill's death, it rang clearly and loudly without a reason. There was no fire; just the one in my heart. It's the permanent one installed by the builder, never needing a change of battery. An odd occurrence indeed and certainly makes one think!

Even 10 years later, the word "widow" still pierces me like a lance. I have trouble saying it, though it's no longer just another word in the English language. For a long time the word "widow" has described me accurately – empty, as its Latin meaning suggests. Alone and empty when I go to bed at night and when I wake in the morning; empty when I eat my meals or go away or return from a holiday. Making decisions, big or small, is a difficult task. At times, the emptiness, the void in my life feels almost total. No longer do I have Bill to rescue me or cheer me on in my performances. He was my biggest fan, my friend, my companion, my lover. Without his support, it is always hard to motivate myself to do even the things I love.

Prior to our marriage, Bill and I had become involved with a ballroom dance group and we continued this for some years, as well as taking up Scottish country dancing when we lived out West. For me, going to a church dance today as a single person is a reminder of Bill's absence. When the slow songs are played, knowing they are only for couples becomes a torture for me. I have "braved the storm" on a few occasions and agonized over the worry I've put my friends through when they watched out for me, not wanting me to be left sitting alone at the table. What a responsibility! On one occasion, guys and gals were called on the floor as Elvis sang, "I Can't Help Falling in Love With You". Every couple went to the dance floor. I was left sitting with 14 empty chairs. Suddenly, my dear friend Jan realized the situation and she made a quick exit to the ladies washroom, as her husband came and rescued me. Out of compassion and kindness comes laughter, and I will always remember their good deed. At the same time, I want my friends to enjoy such precious moments for themselves and not always to feel an obligation to me. Awkward situations are sometimes easier to avoid just by not going. Certainly in our early stages of grief, this is the case. It does get easier.

We often hear that it's a "couple's world", but it's not until we are single that we can really appreciate what this means. Sometimes it's hard to accept the reality. We have to force ourselves not to take it personally when we are left out. Being the "fifth wheel" is not for everyone; though, for the most part, I'm comfortable in the company of my friends, who are very gracious at including me.

About six weeks after Bill's death, I received a gift in the mail from him. Just holding it in my hands made me feel he was still present with me. He knew my love for royalty and for Princess Diana. His gift was a commemorative stamp collection of Her Royal Highness, the Princess of Wales. The gift seemed to come from Heaven and I was elated. I happened to be away at the time of her death. Bill captured every detail of her funeral on video for me to watch on my return. He was well aware of my interest. This wasn't the only gift I was to receive from Bill after his death. Some time later, I found a flyer for a Chicago show in which I'd performed. Bill had had the flyer mounted on a plaque and I expect he'd been saving it for Christmas. Each was an example of his thoughtfulness and love and in the months after his death, I clutched at the idea that I was not entirely alone or without him.

Who was the man Bill Stronach? As described by friend, Rick Goodman in his eulogy:

"Bill was the most warm, friendly, optimistic man that I have ever met. His laugh depicted his approach to life. To Bill, the glass was always half full! He treated each day as it came. He would always listen to you, never being judgmental. He was never critical of anyone. He was a true friend. He was a leader of men, an organizer, a man of values and compassion. He was in love with Enid and his family and he was in love with life. His term of endearment for Enid rings in my ears. "Can I do anything for you 'Luv'? 'Luv', have you seen my glove? 'Luv', where's the rye? 'Luv', can I make you a drink? Bill was willing to try anything once and be there for anyone. To Bill, life was a journey to be experienced."

Tara said "I called him Uncle; to me that's what he was; someone I loved for his kind ways, his smiles, his easy going attitude and his laughter…someone I looked up to for the way he made his family the biggest part of his life." Tara is my cousin's daughter, a delightful young woman, now in her thirties.

The production of Li'l Abner was dedicated to the memory of Bill Stronach. In the company of my friends Jan and Pat, I was able to go and see one of the performances.

Bill Stronach
1946-1997

Bill & Enid

Richard

Winter passed. Snow was shovelled. The dog was walked. "Thank you" notes were written. Christmas happened, but not as usual. Tradition would have been too difficult, so change was necessary. Turkey was barbecued and delicious, but the tears were plentiful. Everything, even small domestic chores seemed to have a weight attached to them and required so much more energy than ever before. Little could I imagine that our lives were going to get a lot sadder and tougher.

Well into March, Bill Sr. was labouring to breathe and now required nursing help. Leaving my boys at home, I drove the two hours to Belleville to spend a weekend with my in-laws. I ventured home early on Sunday evening after a snow storm. Richard and Steven had shovelled our driveway and when I got home we ordered pizza, prior to leaving for Richard's hockey game. This would be his last game of the season, prior to final play-offs. Before we left for the ice rink, the snow plough came around again, making it necessary for

Richard to shovel the heavy late-winter snow from the end of our driveway for the second time so that we could drive the car out.

Taking his equipment with him, Richard entered the Glen Abbey Arena while I parked the car. Bill had been our family's chief hockey fan, never missing a game. Now it was up to Steven and me to give Richard our support. "I love you...score one for Dad," I said to Richard as he walked through the door onto the ice to begin the game. Minutes later my son collapsed and died on the ice. It was March 22nd, 1998, three days after his 17th birthday, and just five months after his father died.

Richard's last birthday cake; we never had the chance to celebrate his 17th birthday.

Richard was very healthy and athletic, with no signs at all that anything might have been wrong. My legs weakened as I came down slowly from the stands to the ice; I was so dazed I had to stop and sit on the stairs for a few minutes in order to maintain my awareness of what was happening. One of the hockey dads was a doctor, one of the moms a nurse. They, with others, immediately attended to Richard. The team captain signalled to call the emergency services and it wasn't long before paramedics arrived. I made my way from the stands, watching my son motionless on the ice and thinking the worst. Could this really be happening? I was too bewildered to be able to take it all in. It wasn't an option for me to go in the ambulance so I went to the hospital in the car of complete strangers, whom I have never heard from again. Later, however, I did track down their names and wrote them in appreciation. At the hospital, my friend Linda arrived. We sat and waited for the horrible, horrible news. My youngest son, Richard, aged 17, was gone too. His hockey team-mates were in the lobby – young people who were all devastated when they were told Richard was dead.

Before leaving the hospital, I was escorted to a room. By now, my good friends Rick and Eleanor, along with our minister and the coroner, were there. Then, the question…did I want to donate Richard's eyes? Looking back, this would have been a wonderful thing to do. How comforting it would be today to know that someone else enjoys the benefit of seeing through Richard's eyes. At the time, so shortly after seeing my son die in front of me, I was in no state to make such a decision or to give my consent. I wasn't ready to accept the reality of my son's death. Giving his eyes would have been too final. For this reason, I am now a strong advocate of mandatory organ donation consent forms being completed prior to issuing a person's driving licence.

Rick and Eleanor drove me home from the hospital, and stayed the night, I think, along with Linda and Bob. Maybe the men went home. So many of those hours remain a blur. My son Steven was out for the evening and it was around midnight, I believe, when he arrived home unaware of the terrible news I was about to break to him. My eyes were red from crying, my face still stricken with shock. As soon as he saw extra cars in the driveway and several of us sitting in the living room, Steven knew that something was horribly wrong. There is no good way to give heart-breaking news to someone you love. I told him the awful truth as simply as I could.

"No, not my brother too!" he cried, disbelieving and shattered. I thought: How are we ever going to survive this one? My heart ached for the loss of my son and husband. And I feared the pain and suffering that lay ahead for Steven and me. I knew that no magic wand would be able to fix or change what we were about to go through. For our parents too, this was unimaginable.

Steven insisted he had to see Richard, so back to the hospital we went. I don't know how we got there. What I do remember is being escorted by two police officers into the room where Richard lay. How dare they not allow us time alone with him. I think we both resented the lack of privacy and felt angry at this thoughtless and callous intrusion on our grief.

My memory isn't clear, but when a young person dies unexpectedly, the police don't rule out drugs or anything else as being the cause of death until tests and an autopsy are completed. After Richard was pronounced dead, the officers asked permission to come to the house to search his room; normal procedure, they said. Of course, I obliged, but they never did come. A congenital heart defect was the cause of death. Anything else was no longer considered.

A few weeks later, I was devastated when I found out the police had cut the lock on Richard's school locker and inspected its contents. That should have been my job; I resented that complete strangers had rifled through his personal possessions. Unknown to me, everything had been returned to the house. After much preparation, I had made arrangements with a favourite teacher of Richard's and a close school friend to go and open the locker. I was shocked and outraged in learning it had been done the morning after his death. No one communicated with me in advance, nor was my permission requested. In a letter to the Chief of Police, I asked for a full explanation as to why this violation of privacy occurred. I would not accept a bureaucratic mix-up as an acceptable reply. My grief counsellor took me to the police station where we met and received an apology from the Chief of Police. Then I had to let it go.

My son's sudden death left a mark on our close-knit community. So many of his friends were at that hockey game and saw him collapse. The tragedy brought forth an outpouring of community support from police, social workers and grief counsellors. Help was offered to everyone who attended the next scheduled game. Instead of playing hockey, team mates, family and friends joined together at the arena where support workers were on hand to help those in need of it, as a result of our tragic loss.

Richard's funeral was big; 700 people filled the church to capacity. Unlike Bill's funeral, I greeted no one, and spoke to no one. I walked out of the church, a car door was open for me to get in, and from there I was chauffeured home. I was numb with shock and have no recollection of the rest of the day. Even Kipper, our Labrador retriever, was howling in grief. Bill had walked him every night for thirteen years. Now that was ended. Kipper had arthritis, so the boys had been carrying him up the stairs every night. Now Richard would no longer be there. So much was changed in our once-happy household. Life as we knew it could never be the same. The day after Richard's funeral, Steven and I said goodbye to another member of our family when we took Kipper to be put to sleep to end his pain. I had called the vet to question Kipper's howling and he confirmed that dogs grieve too. When I asked "If he were your dog, what would you do?" he answered, "I think it's time." Our friend Roy, with his wife, Lexie, had come from Vernon, B.C. to attend Richard's funeral and now Steven and I appreciated Roy's help with Kipper. Bill and Roy had worked together in B.C. in the 1970's and we had become very good friends with him and Lexie, his wife. I'm sure that Kipper is now with Bill and Richard at their new address in Heaven, with only golden stairs to climb.

Now Steven would be without his beloved pet of thirteen years. They were best buddies. His Dad, his little brother and now his dog.

I hope the story about Rainbow Bridge is true. It's just this side of Heaven, and when an animal dies, that's where they go. At Rainbow Bridge, they are restored to health and vigor, enjoying happiness and contentment with all the other animals, except for one small thing; they each miss someone very special to them, who had to be left behind. The day comes when one suddenly stops and looks into the distance. His bright eyes are intent. His eager body quivers. Suddenly he begins to run from the group, flying over the green grass, his legs carrying him faster and faster. You have been spotted, and when you and your special friend finally meet, you cling together in joyous reunion, never to be parted again. The happy kisses rain upon your face; your hands again caress the beloved head, and you look once more into the trusting eyes of your pet, so long gone from your life but never absent from your heart. Then you cross Rainbow Bridge together.

The days and weeks that followed the deaths and funerals were understandably difficult. What I do remember is my dear Dad standing at the kitchen sink, washing dishes constantly. He always seemed to be stuck with that chore, although for him, it was no hardship. Someone commented "Dick, you've been at that sink all day!" to which one of Steven's friends remarked "He's been there all week!" This made us laugh.

Our friend Rick came with me to a paediatric cardiologist. The doctor told us that there were no answers to explain Richard's tragedy. His right coronary artery had been in the wrong place; a congenital heart defect, I was told. The cardiologist called it an anomaly. Had it been a left coronary artery and had it been discovered, doctors might have been able to re-route the artery. Otherwise, a complete heart transplant might have been possible. In any event, a normal life, enjoying all the sports that Richard enjoyed, might not have been possible for my son. But why? Why Richard? And why such a short time after losing his father? There would be no answers, although I tried, and still try to understand and to accept. All was in God's hands. We aren't given any choices.

The autopsy showed a scar on the heart, that there had been a previous heart attack. I recalled that in 1994, I received a phone call from the school, telling me that Richard had fainted, I think while in gym. He was fine, but they felt a responsibility to tell me in order to have him checked by the doctor. Of course, we did this, and ECG tests proved to be normal. It is my understanding that there were no tests that would have shown he had a congenital heart defect. I had to put my trust in the medical experts. To this day, I wonder if that fainting spell was a slight heart attack. I will never know the answer to that.

A few years later, defibrillators were placed in strategic areas around the community. The recreation facility where Richard died was one of them. The odds of survival are almost four times greater if someone performs CPR immediately. When combined with early defibrillation, survival rates can increase by 50% or more if delivered in the first few minutes. Would Richard have lived if there had been a defibrillator at the arena in 1998? I will never know the answer to that either.

Before Richard took his last few steps on the ice, and as he sat on the bench with his team mates, he had apparently said "I feel like my heart is going to jump right out of my chest!" His coach directed him to sit out, but then he felt better enough to go back onto the ice. Time and time again, Richard's words play over in my head, especially when I feel a heart palpitation or slight flutter in my chest. I think of the anxiety he must have felt as he looked up into the stands and didn't see his dad cheering him on. How difficult that must have been for him, and could that have had anything to do with his sudden passing? I could flog myself to death trying to resolve things that there are simply no answers for.

For a long time, I felt so much anger towards God. How can there even be a God who allows such things to happen, I thought? This test of my faith would be something I had to work through on my own. It would take months and years before I could understand and accept how God makes His presence known. I was once asked, "If God told you that you would be blessed with a beautiful son, but only for 16 years. After that time, He would take him back. Would you still want him?" Of course, the answer was simple. I was happy to have had Richard for the time we shared together. Coping with his death, so soon after his dad's death, was impossible. But over time, I was presented with circumstances, situations and answers that provided me with small and gradual moments of hope that have allowed me to move forward. There were those inevitable moments when someone came into my life at precisely the right time, and said or did precisely the right thing. I liked to believe that these people were human angels who appeared when I most needed guidance, strength and support. Words of comfort from a book, a timely phone call, a significant dream, an unexpected visitor, a pleasant surprise, have occurred as if sent from Heaven. These synchronous happenings have me trusting that there is more to my life than what I experience on a physical level. I accept the fact that there is more to my experiences than immediately meets the eye. All have had so much meaning, and happened so coincidentally, that I have gradually changed my thinking. Faith would get me through these terrible ordeals. So, I have learned to put my trust in God.

Floral arrangement from hockey team;
16 was the number on Richard's jersey.

Celebrating a Life

Richard was gone, but the hockey final play-off game took place about ten days after his death. How hard it was to watch that game. Without Richard on the ice, the arena looked empty. The emotional tension was enormous. I felt so stricken by longing for my lost son that my legs and arms were numb. My body seemed to belong to someone else. My mind flashed back to that night, so few days before, when I'd sat and watched in terror and disbelief my son Richard collapsing on the ice. Despite the agony of attending the play-off game, I was determined to support Richard's team and I was glad that Steven and I made the effort.

The M.O.H.A. (Minor Oaks Hockey Association) Moms were most kind and caring as they gave me my instructions to proceed onto the ice after the game to make the presentation. The 1997-98 memorial trophy went to a classmate of Richard's.

All his team-mates wore his number 16 over their hearts. With Richard with them in spirit, his team won the game, though their justifiable jubilation was touched with sadness; Richard was to have been presented with Best Defenseman of the League. This would have been quite an honour; one that has been presented to a Midget Red player every year since then. It is now called the Rich Stronach Memorial. The trophy has a home at River Oaks Arena, which I visit often. The play-off game and memorial presentation is held every March. My cousin's daughter, Tara and husband Brent have never missed, and for this I am very grateful. For Steven and me, it is so much a memorial to our beloved son and brother. Steven has never been able to come on the ice with me to make the presentation. Some day he may feel more ready to do this. I do it for Richard, regardless of the emotions it stirs up.

Each year, the recipient of the award receives a note of congratulations from me, along with the presentation photo. After one of these occasions, in 2006, the boy sent me a lovely card. He said he hadn't been aware of the significance of the award at the time. They had lost the game and that had been his focus. Now, he told me he realized, "other things that night mattered more than winning the game". I wanted to acknowledge his card, but struggled with taking this any further. Maybe I should leave it alone. But when I read the "Daily Word" I knew I was meant to write to him. The message for the day was, "A sincere thank-you, spoken quietly or written in a note, is appreciation that I share from my heart for people who have blessed me. Thank-you's move out from me in every direction to many people. I leave no one out." So my dilemma was resolved and I wrote him back. A coincidence? Of course not.

Many floral tributes came for Richard. The one from the hockey team was large, heart-shaped with red roses, in the shape of number 16, the number Richard wore on his jersey. The card read "Dedicated to the memory of Rich Stronach, a great combination of talent, heart and determination we shall not see soon again. With love from your Red Wing Team Mates."

Seventeen red roses came from Shannon, his girlfriend. He had just turned seventeen. Richard's friends at high school put together a showcase with special memorabilia. The student council purchased a tree that now grows outside the west entrance to the school. Wilf Goodman, our friend Rick's father, donated an ash tree from his Vanaheim Tree Farm and when the tree was planted in the park behind the school the occasion was well attended by his friends and teachers. Rick, Eleanor and all the Goodman family have been an on-going support for me; they treat me like family. Alison Goodman handed out blue ribbons, which were tied on the tree. Both trees in my son's memory are thriving. I visit them often.

A note received from a teacher at Richard's high school told me that unfortunately, she never had the chance to know Richard. However, many of her students had known him well. When she was trying to think of a way to change the speech patterns of her students, they suggested paying ten cents every time they said "like". They also suggested the money be donated in Richard's memory. They sent their cheque to the Heart & Stroke Foundation. She said I had a very special son and he is missed.

It's true…Richard was a sweet and gentle soul, so very much like my Dad. At age sixteen, their likeness in appearance is uncanny. You would think you were looking at the same person. Our genes are a remarkable thing.

A favourite memory of Richard's sweetness always comes to mind. We had been to the vet with his hamster and found out it had a tumor. I found this note under Richard's pillow with his tooth attached to it. It reads "Dere tothfairy..Plese giv me $25 because I need it for an nedel to maybey get red of his tomor. Heres my toth. Prity Plese $25." Spelling wasn't his priority, and not his teacher's either as the focus was phonics (sounding it out).

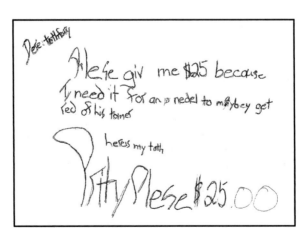

We weren't able to save the hamster. I remember him taking it in a shoebox to bury it in the trail.

Twenty six friends and family returned to the campground where we had spent so many wonderful summer holidays. There, we had a memorial service for Bill and Richard and, of course, Kipper. We scattered some of their ashes. Our camping friends presented me with a painting of Lookout Point, Blind Bay, where we'd hiked on many occasions. It was there that we would stop to rest, swim with the dogs and snack on treats from our backpacks. It seemed an appropriate resting place for their ashes.

Everyone signed the back of the painting and it hangs now in my sitting room. I will always cherish it as a keepsake of their love for Bill and Richard.

With the help of Shannon, Richard's girlfriend, we chose a PD day to invite school friends to help themselves to his treasures. They arrived sporadically throughout the day. I gave them the details of his death, let them look through his photo album and see the various newspaper articles about him.

The night before his friends came to the house, I had a significant dream and it wasn't long before I had this explained and was ready to share with all, especially Shannon and her family. Without realizing it at the time, the day happened to be Good Friday. Of course, the day was very emotional.

My dream focused on Richard's friends coming to see his bedroom and his things for the last time. Shannon's young sister, Jamie, seemed to be in the fore. Of course, I wondered if I was receiving a strong message from Richard not to forget Jamie. I had never met Jamie, and therefore had not given a thought to her coming to the house on that day. When she arrived at the door with her mom and sister the next morning, I was elated and couldn't hold back the tears. Richard's wishes had been answered. Jamie was very fond of Richard, as he was of her. I relayed my dream to them and when Jamie finally found the courage to go upstairs to Richard's room, she chose a pink stuffed pig as a keepsake. Later, we laughed through our tears because, of all things, there had been a reference to bacon in my dream. It wasn't until afterwards that we put this all together, and were amazed by the coincidence. I believe that if we leave ourselves open, clearly, we can receive messages from the spirit world.

My mother slept in my bed for weeks after the deaths of Bill and Richard. I cried myself to sleep. She comforted me with a healing touch and often cried with me. These were terrible days. No one knew what to say or do. We were stunned, overcome by the shock and by sadness. Sometimes friends included me in dinner parties and outings but always my mind was elsewhere. Over the weeks, Steven became withdrawn, as if protecting himself from the world that had attacked us so mercilessly. Alcohol and drugs eased the pain temporarily when it was all too much for him to face head on. At that time Steven wasn't ready to accept that loss and grief are inevitable parts of the human experience. In my own journey through grief, I've learned that accepting death and the pain that comes when loved ones are taken from us is the only way to live through overwhelming loss. Nurturing care would have come to Steven, if he had wanted it. It has been my good fortune to discover, through prayer and the gifts of friends and counselling, that sharing grief allows us to ease our burden by letting someone else help us to carry it. For many reasons, Steven had to keep his sorrow buried deep inside his chest. No one could reach him while in such pain.

The encouragement I received from friends was what got me out of bed on many occasions. "Get in the shower!" they would say. They were coming over with lunch. Then they would organize an outing with more friends to Niagara on the Lake. Off we'd go for the day; they were there for comfort when my defences were down.

Richard's friends, mostly the girls, came to visit in small groups. Shannon, Richard's girlfriend and I went out together for lunch and reminisced. Richard had been very close to Shannon's family. They were good to him. Richard's friends got together on their own and, on one occasion, went to Kilbear, the campground where we had spent so many wonderful family summer holidays. They went to the jumping rocks and other places they remembered. They took some pictures and returned home. When they picked up the pictures, there was one extra photograph they had not taken; it was a vision of a male figure, standing by a tree at the jumping rocks where they'd once played. The boys were convinced this was Richard's spirit. He was there with them...what a comforting thought. Those boys missed their friend. My family would never forget seeing a good buddy of Richard's on the day of his funeral, sitting alone on the curb, head in hands, buried in grief. Such loss would be traumatic for any 16-year-old. To this day, my aunt recalls the grief-stricken boy on the curb.

Bill, Enid and Richard - 1995

Two boys wrote poetry in their friend's memory.
One was called:

"Can You Take Me Higher"

Once upon a time, a hawk flew free
Without one care in the world but friends and hockey
Now the time is gone where a simple handshake is
felt
Words to this can only be spelt
His family and friends will never forget
The charming smiles and loving wit
Once upon a time, a hawk flew free
The day is not felt where you cannot still see
Loving you Rich Stronach
Always and forever

Enid Stronach is the most courageous, passionate
and loving person that I have ever known. Rich will
always know the unconditional love we all have for
him.
To one of the best friends I have ever had
We'll see each other again some day.
Rich loved and looked up to Steve with all his heart.
I never heard one bad thought from Rich about him.
He can still see you, Steve, and he would want you to
be strong.
You were a very happy part of Rich's life. This I
know.
He loves you very much.
He is proud to have such a loving brother, and you
know this.
Keep strong."
By: Brad Armstrong

At the time, our emotions were burning; no one could have imagined experiencing such a tragedy, a double whammy so to speak. I expect this is why Brad (Richard's friend) spoke so highly of me…as if I was as courageous as Wonder Woman. Nevertheless, I do appreciate his kind words.

The poem from the other friend had very moving words but no title:

"Time and change as life goes on
With each new day, a different song
We've lost some friends down the road
Here's the story and how it's told
As time passed, well, so did he
And I'm just left with memories
He got me through when times were dim
I couldn't have made it without him
But still, without him life goes on,
I will continue, head high, stead strong
So friends passed will see I'm strong.
Lessons learned keep me strong,
As time goes by, I will carry on,
With memories held close to my heart,
I send them to you each night in my thoughts,
Hoping for a sign that your strength has carried on
Because without your strength I couldn't carry on.
In terms of replacement, this is important.
In haunting form, the same old smile;
A life he filled with great assortment;
We still see you bro', but it's been a while.
How was your weekend?"

The boy who wrote this poem had been a friend of Richard's but, as always between good friends, they had also had their differences. Soon after  Richard's death, he had a tattoo put on his arm with the initials RNS (Richard Neil Stronach), with red hearts and green ivy. Richard obviously had a special place in his heart. I let him know how deeply touched I was, and that what he'd done was very meaningful to those of us who knew and loved Richard so much. The tattoo will be a constant reminder. It says a thousand words; their friendship must have been a strong one. I told him Richard would be very moved if he knew what his friend had done. It gives me great comfort to believe Richard does know and that he watches over us always.

Two other friends also have tattoos with Richard's initials and dates, 1981-1998. When I suggested to one of the boys that this was permanent (with the  thought of regret in my head), he replied, "That's why I did it!" I think each of us makes our own private memorial.

Tibetan symbol for "spirit"

A most welcome e-mail arrived many years later from a school friend of Richard's. He had been talking with his Dad and reminiscing about elementary school. It didn't take long for Richard's name to come up, and before they knew it, they were sharing memories about street hockey games and stories of dents in his Dad's garage that were courtesy of himself and Richard as they developed their 4th and 5th grader slap shots…needless to say, missing the net more often than not. His Dad told him I had written a book, which prompted him to contact me. He now lives out west and was here for only a short time. I was delighted to have his company that afternoon, as well as hearing the stories about fun times enjoyed by he and Richard. These surprise visits are most welcome and somehow present themselves just when I need a lift. We talked a lot about moving forward after difficulties and tragedies, which brought to mind for him the word 'Surgite' that an academic advisor at university had presented to him when he was having difficulty with focus and studies. After a poor start to his post-secondary life at university, this was the given message, which indeed, he has not forgotten. It is the Latin meaning for 'push on'. As the story goes, Sir Isaac Brock told his soldiers to "Surgite!" This was his last word as he was killed in action during the Battle of 1812. Yes indeed, "push on" is what we must do, despite our trials.

Richard's friend told me that in the years between 2001 and 2008, he trained over 1,000 town staff and public in the operation of Automated External Defibrillators (AED's) and the science behind them. He told me he thought about

Richard more than a few times while teaching those courses. On a positive note, he said it was nice to know that his teaching might make a difference in a future incident, possibly saving a life.

One of the newspaper articles in *The Oakville Beaver* was entitled, "Remembering Richard Stronach". It reads as follows:

"Seventeen year old Richard Stronach from Glen Abbey, passed away Sunday evening, doing what he loved best. The lively young hockey player collapsed on the ice at the Glen Abbey Rec Centre, after just completing his shift at the close of the second period. He was rushed to Oakville Trafalgar Memorial Hospital. A post mortem determined the Blakelock student died as a result of a congenital heart defect.

A long time member of the Minor Oaks Hockey Association, Richard Stronach was highly thought of by both players and coaches. Marshall Snowball, VP of MOHA House League had nothing but high praise for Richard. "Rich was a kid who loved the game," said Snowball this week. "I coached him on last year's Bantam Select Team, and what I remember about him most was how intense he was, and very competitive. A natural leader with great skills. He was always one of the top defensemen in the league. In my 28 years of coaching, he was one of the best. I would have been proud to have him on any team of mine."

Snowball remembers Richard as a self-motivated boy, with lots of drive. Mike Zardo, president of the MOHA, never coached Richard, but certainly knew his reputation. "He was a very talented hockey player," recalled Zardo.

Zardo, who was at the rink on Sunday night, recognized how difficult Richard's death is for both the coaches and the players. "We are all grieving; it is a very difficult situation. I would like to say that our wishes and prayers are with Richard's family at this time."

Richard himself, along with his mom Enid and older brother Steven were still coping with the untimely death of Bill Stronach in October of last year.

Barb Nevins' family has been Roxborough Drive neighbours with the Stronachs since 1984. "I always had a special place in my heart for Richard." Barb recalled, "He had a smile that would melt your heart." She added, "Sunny. Rich was sunny."

Barb, who has three sons of her own including Michael, who is the same age as Rich, remembers Richard as always on his way to some sort of sport.

The Canadian flag is flying at half-mast at Blakelock School, where Rich attended grade eleven. Grief counsellors have been in the school all this week helping kids to deal with his loss. "He was a very popular boy," said Barb."

Richard's friends have survived and, inevitably and properly, their lives have moved on. However, all their outpourings of their love for my son and for my husband have been, and continue to be, a great source of inspiration and support to both Steven and myself.

One year later would have been Richard's graduating year. I was invited to attend, which I did, and although it was very emotional seeing Richard's picture up on the screen with his many pals, I think he would have been proud that I went. These events are draining, but years later, I'm happy that I attended.

For some friends of Richard's, it took a number of years before they were able to contact me. One boy came around the anniversary of Richard's death, and with Easter approaching, he had an Easter lily for me. Such a nice gesture I thought, and he was most pleased to leave with one of Richard's hockey jerseys as a keepsake.

I especially cherish particular keepsakes. One of them is an art project Richard had done in class. His art teacher kindly had it framed and brought it to me. Now it has pride of place hanging just outside his room. She included a letter in which she explained that the Grade 10 project was based on an understanding of the historical art style called surrealism and an exploration of the drawing technique called perspective. The technical skill of perspective shows the ability to draw depth. Students were to include a checker board or stairs in their drawings and to show them realistically. Surrealism shows dreams and fantasy, generally showing dreamlike images, which could not be real, in realistic ways. Richard's picture shows sky and clouds through an open door in a realistic way.

It all seemed so uncanny. Richard's death seemed surreal and the art style was called surrealism. His picture was of our front door, looking out, to the clouds and sunshine. Richard was a ray of sunshine to all who knew him. His friends made a memorial video, which they presented to me soon after his death. I admit it's hard to watch. This was another way that friends found to deal with their grief. They spoke to Richard in the video as if he were still with them.

It was also heart-warming to receive phone calls from Richard's teachers, who spoke so highly of him. For some time after his death, I got together for lunch with one teacher who was particularly good to my son. It was encouraging to share remembrances, and to know that Richard was so well thought of.

Long after the funeral and memorial service, my mom and I sat at her dining table for hours re-living the countless kindnesses people shared after Richard's death, some by people we didn't even know. People who had lost a child came forward with notes of condolence. So many sent flowers, donations or food. I have been in touch with everyone to acknowledge their thoughtfulness and compassion. I wrote hundreds of thank-you notes.

To this day, eleven years later, the pain of losing my son is overwhelming. Tears are running down my cheeks as I re-live the nightmare of that horrible time and write these words. Yet how true it is that journalizing is therapeutic. I encourage anyone who grieves to put pen to paper to write about their experience and feelings. Until a person allows her or himself to feel the gut-wrenching pain of loss, the complete disorientation, anger and sadness, it is difficult to get to the other side of grief and to move forward with their life. They don't call it "grief work" for nothing. I am still in that process; though I have been blessed with the capability to reach out to other people and to discover strengths I never knew I possessed. I once heard Mary Tyler Moore say that we are given breath, so inevitably, we carry on. She too had lost a son, and the interviewer had asked her "How does anyone survive after the loss of a child?"

I have benefited from a lot of counselling, and have learned much about the journey of grief. I know it is never easy. I joined a group of bereaved moms, all bearing the pain of losing a child. Bereavement means "to be robbed." (The leader of this group lost her husband and three sons and later passed away herself in August of 2007. She wrote two short books about her grief journey.) Some women had also lost their spouse. They were good women…kindred spirits in my time of need, and we were pleased to have each other's support. We also knew we had to set our own paths, while realizing that there is no way to pretend that working through grief is easy. We agreed that we don't resolve the death or deaths, but instead, learn to realign ourselves to our new, unwelcome realities. It takes huge, heaving effort.

One of these grieving moms wrote:

"You can't imagine the comfort it gives to the sorrowing parents. It is a place of safety. Countless times our members say "Thank God for this group—I was close to suicide". And I thank God also that He works through us to give courage and strength to others and in return we are made stronger."

Another mom wrote:

"My Friday Friends…
It's been 2 years since I joined the Friday morning club
We meet around the table; we try to cheer each other up
We tell each other stories, some happy and some sad
All our feelings flow out, about the loved ones that we had
It's been 2 years since I joined the Friday morning club
There were times we've laughed, there were times we cried
There were times we have hugged over people who have died
But one thing's certain, one thing's true,
I could not have gotten through this if it hadn't been for you
It's been 2 years since I met my friends who gather here
They hold your hand and understand the troubles that you share
So here's to old friends and to new who gather at this place
Let us remain together in health and God's Grace
To my friends around this table my coffee cup I raise

To you and your loved ones, may we all see brighter days

For you have brightened my life by just being you

So smart and so funny, good friends through and through."

We loved the Black-eyed Susans
on Kal Mountain, Vernon, B.C.
Enid, Richard, Steven

Baby Face

Little Captain

Richard Stronach
1981—1998

Handsome Fellow

Proud Standard Bearer
at the Canadian Open

Grief, Dreams and Angels

During the same month my son died, my Uncle Jack had a heart attack. Thankfully he survived but, as we were his only next of kin, trying to juggle responsibilities became quite challenging. Although I can't recall details, I do remember my girlfriends assisting at that time.

Almost one month after my son Richard died, and six months after Bill died, my father-in-law also passed away. Could this be real? How would I cope with yet another funeral? Where would I gain the strength? Steven and I just missed grandpa's passing by a short time at the hospital. Now we had another funeral to prepare for. At Bill and Richard's funerals, the closing hymn was the lovely "Go Now in Peace", so it seemed appropriate to sing it at Bill Sr.'s funeral service in Belleville. I still feel a pang today as we sing it at the end of every Sunday service. I also sang solo the Lord's Prayer, accompanied by the organ. To this day, I don't know how I accomplished that without breaking down. It was in Someone else's hands, and I got through it.

All three generations gone. Nana had lost her son, her grandson, and now her husband, in six months. Steven lost his father, his brother, his dog, and now his Grandpa. My world had collapsed totally. Life seemed dangerous and worthless. All I wanted to do was to cry and to stay in bed. Fortunately, I still had Steven, as well as my parents and my mother-in-law who needed me. Although we were all shattered, somehow we managed to remain strong for each other.

Around the time my son died, a woman who had lost a child along with her mother at their cottage captured a picture of a cloud formation that looked like an angel with arms outreached holding a baby. It was a comforting picture for this family, who marketed it and sold thousands across the country. I was gifted one; it hangs in my kitchen and reminds me daily that my loved ones are safe with the angels.

Intense feelings of grief can hit us at any time. I remember one night at our Among Friends Dinner Club, which Bill and I had always enjoyed so much. It was the annual ornament exchange at Christmas time. It was my turn to choose, and upon opening the packet in my lap I found an angel. My delight soon turned to apprehension when I realized anyone else was free to take the angel from me as the dinner game progressed. My throat and stomach were in knots, as I feared my angel might be taken from me. There were fifteen of us and if someone had "stolen" my angel - and they were certainly entitled to do so - I think the last of any strength remaining in me would also have been robbed. That night is still torture for me when I recall the feelings of panic and anxiety. I still fear loss in any form.

One day as I drove in my car, a song by Amy Sky came on the radio. The timing was perfect. The words were, "If my heart had wings, I'd fly to the sky and bring back all the love that's missing from my life. Heaven's Angels have come to lead the way." I went out and bought the CD right away. Fantasizing about my loved ones coming back gave me something else to think about, other than their deaths. Amy Sky also wrote, "Tell Me It's Not True", a sad but very pretty song from the Broadway show, Blood Brothers. I attended her concert and then wrote to her explaining the impact that her music had on me. She also wrote a song and sang it at Barbara Underhill's last skating exhibition after the death of Barb's daughter. Barb was also at the concert that evening in Oakville.

Another afternoon, I was driving away from my house with friends Linda and Barb when we saw a goose and a duck sitting on the boulevard across the street. We thought it was very odd. Linda said, "It's Bill and Richard." I grasped onto that thought. I'm sure we've all heard stories about life after death and speculated what creature we might want to return as. I think it's healthy to find humour in sad situations and I accepted the duck and goose waddling on the lawn, chuckling at life, just as Bill and Richard would have done, as an amusing and comforting fantasy. My friend Betty lost her 8-year-old son to cancer. There was a ladybug present after he passed, so now that small and lovely creature has great significance to her family. When they see a ladybug, it's like a visit from their son. Another friend, George, recently lost his wife and a day or two after she died, a hawk landed on the birdbath in their backyard. To George, this was his beloved wife's watchful eyes looking out for him. Events such as these bring a small amount of comfort after the loss of a loved one. These synchronous happenings are more than random occurrences, and if we look at them more closely, they can show us that the universe is listening and gently communicating with us. Learning to pay attention to and link the things that occur on a daily basis can be a way for us to become more attuned to the fact that most everything happens in our lives for a reason, even when that reason is not clear right away.

In July of 1998, just four months after my son's death, I was reading "Talking to Heaven". The section on dreams said that the easiest way for us to reach spirits while we're sleeping is to think about our passed loved ones before falling asleep. Thinking about my husband and my son was a constant, so occasionally I did dream about them.

My first dream was more like a nightmare. I was in bed when I heard someone trying to break in through my ensuite bathroom window. I got up, saw a fair-haired man at the window and tried to call 911. I panicked and struggled hard, using every bit of my strength and energy to keep the window closed and the man out. There was a tree on the front lawn and also a white get-away van parked close by. I managed to shut the window.

My friend Andrea arrived and told me, "The Lord is With You". Then a police woman appeared without being called. I woke agitated and weak.

A short time later, my friend Andrea from Vernon, B.C., arrived in person. She was able to take me to meet her brother Bruce and his wife Maryanne. Both have a Masters degree in psychology and social work and had studied dreams. Their interpretation of the symbolism in my dream was interesting. They explained it this way:

The open window was my vulnerability and pain.
The blonde man was my son Richard.
The white coloured van symbolized purity, divine light and Richard's dying.
The tree was a symbol for growth.
The main emotion in my dream was fear; my fear of the man getting inside might symbolize my fear of allowing myself to feel the pain and depth of my grief. It might mean that I was not yet ready to experience my pain.

Andrea's brother and sister-in-law talked about my fragility, and the fact that my mind/psyche was protecting me. Feeling the depth of my pain and sorrow might be too scary for me. I had many things on my mind, i.e. caring for my mom and dad, my mother-in-law, my son, an uncle who was sick and for whom my parents and I were his only next of kin, another uncle who was grieving the loss of his wife, and also, all the thank-you notes I had ahead of me. I felt that so many people needed me and depended on me that there was no time for my own needs, my own pain. For example, I felt I should be going back to Belleville to support my mother-in-law who was now on her own. I needed to take care of all these things and more. But as all these pressures built up, I became less and less able to make decisions for myself.

Andrea gave me a stark warning, one I was not keen to hear. All my life I'd taken care of and supported other people, as wife, mother and teacher. Now I was being told that if I kept myself busy for the next year, if I didn't allow myself time for grief work, time to feel the true depth of my pain and, instead stayed on the surface, skirting around it, I could end up seriously depressed. Not only had I lost Bill and Richard, I had also lost my role as wife and mother. I needed time to re-identify myself.

Later, I came to understand that my role as a mother had not vanished, but was forever changed. Richard, at his young age, and still in school, needed guidance in a mothering way. Steven was far from wanting me to mother him, although I will always play that role in his life.

That same day, while visiting Andrea's relatives, they shared a metaphor for me to think about. On an airplane, they always tell you to put on your own oxygen mask first, before helping someone else. Yet here I was trying to help everyone else before looking after my own (oxygen) needs first. No wonder I often felt so tense and stressed that I could not breathe. I also learned that it was important to make weekly appointments with my grief counsellor for guidance and support in working through my grief process. "Work your other commitments around your own grief work," Andrea said to me. She is my friend and also a Palliative Care Educator and home care nurse, and I'm so glad I've trusted her guidance.

During Andrea's visit, she practiced therapeutic touch on me. She explained that Therapeutic Touch and Healing Touch are ways of working with the energy system of the body. Energy moves in us along meridians. It comes from universal energy and flows in and out of us in a balanced way. We all have an aura of our own energy. This energy then flows in and out of us through chakras like a vortex. When physical, emotional, mental or spiritual problems/issues come about in us, our chakras get blocked and our energy system becomes unbalanced. This can lead to disease, etc. Healing Touch works with the chakras/energy to balance the flow. The healer is not actually doing the healing, but rather acts as a channel for the healing to take place on whatever level it needs to. Even if the person doesn't really believe in or feel the effect after, there is still healing taking place. The effects after treatments may be felt very subtly and over time, even more.

Andrea is always a comforting presence, a supportive mentor who has helped me express myself by listening to my thoughts and feelings. She gives me strength and bolsters my spirit as she helps me through the challenges I am faced with. She brought with her a gift, 'Circle of Friends' made out of clay; four people, arms entwined with a white candle in the centre. For me, it was my family circle, still united in a spiritual way. We sat quietly, watching the glow of the candlelight on the figurines. I felt like I could pick out the faces of Bill, Richard, Steven and myself. There was sadness, knowing that Bill and Richard aren't part of our family circle in our physical world. I now needed to know more about them in the spiritual world. Andrea was helpful in guiding me to reading material that I took comfort in.

It was easy to suppress or run away from the often gut-wrenching pain of grief work by distracting myself, but I had to make time in the coming months to do my own grief work before I could help and support others, especially my son Steven.

I had a visit from another wonderful Vernon friend. I recall so well my inability to even pack a few things in a suitcase so we could spend a couple of days at a cottage. Something as simple as deciding what to wear was a difficult focus, especially when we were trying to meet a time deadline in which to leave. With obvious concern, Sue very kindly said "Now, we are just going to stop this and slow down, no pressure; we'll go when we're ready." This seemed to lighten the burden of decision making.

It was now August, and time for my Uncle Jack to move into a retirement home, so, of course, more energy was needed in lending him a hand. Although I was involved with my parents in helping him adjust, we just weren't able, physically or emotionally, to do all we would have liked.

Richard had been gone only five months, and we were still raw in our grief.

I was being pulled in two directions; my counsellor urging me to commit to work through my grief; my dreams seemed to be telling me that I was not yet ready and that I was protecting myself by helping others. Somehow I would have to resolve this painful dilemma before it broke me apart. In looking back, this conflict must have resolved itself. I remember my Uncle Stuart one day asking me, "How would you eat an elephant?" He had to tell me. "One bite at a time." And so, I took his advice. He was a minister, always willing and ready to offer words of wisdom. I miss him.

My life is full, sometimes too full, but we know what they say about a busy person, and that's me, who always finds time to fit something in. It is important for me to stay connected with the people I love and care about. After all, they've loved and cared for me for some time. Reaching out to others has been a focus for me; I would have enjoyed a role as a nurse, but not in our medical system today. I am happy doing my own thing, with a particular interest and focus on the elderly. Elderly people are often unable to speak for themselves. As a result, their needs can be easily missed, with tragic outcomes. Just a wee visit, a phone call, or outing for a meal can bring joy to them, as well as to me!

We were saddened again, after the death of my dear Uncle Jack in June of 1999. My aunt, the love of his life had predeceased him some years earlier. Happily, they are together again.

Bill Stronach Sr.
1921-1998

1981 Enid's parents'
visit to Vernon, B.C.

1982 Bill's parents'
visit to Vernon, B.C.

Practical Problems

In addition to the anguish of grief and loneliness, there are a thousand and one practical problems to be faced after the death of a spouse. Yet the reality of this can be slow to dawn. Overwhelmed by the shock of sudden death, I seemed to live for weeks in a daze in which day-to-day concerns did not exist or ceased to have any relevance whatsoever. Merely going on living, attending funerals, dealing with people – while at the same time attempting to absorb the truth that my beloved Bill and Richard would never return to me – seemed accomplishment enough.

However, although to a person grieving, the world may seem to have stopped completely; to everyone else, the world goes on spinning much as before. Work must be done. Bills have to be paid. Day to day chores that seemed so effortless before have to be taken care of. I know that for some people, after the death of their spouse, the ordinary obligations of the world can break over their heads with cold-hearted and horrifying reality. With the main breadwinner of the family gone, the practical problems can become insurmountable.

Thankfully, my husband left us financially comfortable. I cannot imagine how much more impossible and devastating life might have been for us if we had also been forced to move from our home. However lonely I felt in our house without my Bill, it was still our home, our refuge from a world in which Steven, Richard and I were struggling to reorient ourselves. We were surrounded by what was familiar. Our friends were close by. How different things might have been had Bill not decided to take out mortgage insurance. Because of his prudent care for us, what was owing on our home was taken care of, though not without a long delay while the insurance company tried every pretext to get out of paying. Until that cheque arrived, I lived in constant anxiety, with many sleepless nights, of what the future might hold. Today, I try not to waste time worrying about where my next dollar is coming from. I live on the capital and hope it lasts. What I spend won't be replenished, as once it was, by a regular wage coming in. If I have learned anything through my journey of grief, it is that every moment of life is precious and must be enjoyed and not wasted. Sometimes I do worry a little that the income from the capital will not be enough, but then, as I have learned in a very painful way, none of us can see far ahead in life. We can never know what's going to happen next.

To know that my sons and I were safe in our home was a great comfort in the weeks and months after Bill's death. Even then, there was still so much to attend to in the way of finances, income tax, etc., which I knew nothing about. Paying the monthly bills came easily, as I had been used to doing that. However, the more intricate details of our finances were to me like the mountains and gorges of an unknown landscape through which I was obliged to hike if my sons and I were going to survive. Everywhere I called, people required me to tell them, "my husband died". To get those words out of my mouth was torture. Then it was necessary to provide the death certificate in order to make any changes to accounts or records. However, I tackled each new chore one at a time, often with some nervousness, and took delight at being able to cross each item off my list. I had much assistance and direction from our friend Bob Lingard in compiling a list of all the necessary financial duties that required attention. He made sure I did the work myself, which helped me build my self-confidence in dealing with these matters. But he kept close tabs on the progress I made until everything was completed.

Taking care of even small chores, which before had seemed so effortless, can become daunting challenges. They no longer seem important or "real" when the only reality that matters is the loss of the spouse and child. One of my friends failed to take the garbage out for months after her husband died. She left it in the garage until the smell became foul. I was able to relate to this; so many things no longer mattered. It was a matter of surviving from one day to the next and dealing with what had to be done the best I could at the time.

Bill had looked after the banking account of the hockey team. It contained only $14 but I wanted to close it and pass the money to the president of the hockey association. When I went to the bank the young man behind the counter said he wouldn't do it, that probate would be required. For $14? I was so disappointed and overcome with emotion that I got up and left, feeling very deflated. However, my mom had been a bank employee herself for 30 years, and she knew the manager of the branch. So, after a quick phone call, the manager closed the account and handed me the $14 without question. Of course, the young man was going by the rules but he was also exercising no common sense, considering the circumstances. For the most part, people were very accommodating and understanding. For example, my son was near completing his drivers licence. Young Drivers very kindly returned the fee, with a note of condolence. I donated the money to the Veterinary College at the University of Guelph. I thought Richard would like that. The letter from the Dean wished me comfort in knowing that the donation to the Pet Trust fund in Richard's memory would contribute to the health and well-being of companion animals in the future. Instances such as in the bank happened only occasionally, but when they did, they only served to deepen the frustration, disorientation and sense of utter loss. Sometimes I returned home at the end of the day despairing that I would ever be able to navigate all the obstacles and challenges that arose after Bill's and Richard's deaths.

Every time I drive up to an intersection, I still recall one of the things Richard learned at driving school. When pulling up to a four-way intersection, he kept a distance of one car length from where most people stop. When I asked him why, he said that if someone came up behind him and failed to stop, they would push him right into the intersection. This way, he was allowing extra room in case of mishap. It made sense, and he took his instruction very seriously.

For months, there seemed to be so many different things I had to accomplish on my own for the first time. I did a lot of things too soon, before I was really ready. However, looking back, I now recognize that I was very brave to take on the challenges I did. Most of the time I was weary because of emotional exhaustion.

It was seven or eight years before I was able to make the phone call to arrange to donate Richard's hockey and soccer trophies. They weren't much use to me sitting in a box so I gave the hockey trophies to the Minor Oaks Hockey Association, where they could be used for Special Olympics. I handed over Richard's soccer trophies, in a flood of tears, to the Oakville Soccer Club and I'm glad that other children are now able to benefit from the awards my son received.

I have also completed the task of looking at and sorting through many hundreds of slides of our own and also my parents. When downsizing, it becomes impossible to store so many things that take up much room. This way, I was able to keep the meaningful ones, and dispose of the rest. A very big job indeed, but at the same time, such a feeling of accomplishment.

One "first" that stands out in my mind was going out west after Bill died. This time, he wouldn't be there to meet me as I stepped off the plane.

When we moved out West in 1974, I travelled alone. Although there were rules about security, Bill had made his way right out to the plane. He undoubtedly wanted to give me a warm welcome as I disembarked with our new baby, Steven. Because of my high blood pressure, I had been unable to travel until Steven was three weeks old, so Bill had to go ahead of me. I had yet to see the house Bill had been working on so hard, painting and getting ready for our arrival.

It was difficult to leave our families when we moved out West, but Bill and I soon adjusted to western living and stayed in B.C. for ten years where we made solid friendships. After six years in North Vancouver we transferred to Vernon in the Okanagan Valley, which we also thoroughly enjoyed. Richard was born there in 1981. In 1983 we transferred back east to Oakville. Soon after that we got our dog Kipper. We already had Pinky, our white cat, who lived for 21 years. He came to us when we were married.

In the months after Bill and Richard's deaths, help and support had a strange way of arriving just when I needed it. Sometimes it was just what I needed to move me forward on the path. In

Toronto airport, on my way to Vancouver, I lined up with everyone else for the next available check-in clerk. The reservation clerk called me over. She was a sorority sister and knew me. Very kindly she said she would upgrade my seat. I thanked her through my tears. I was so surprised and delighted that I looked for the nearest telephone to call my mom. When I explained what had happened, she said that my angels were at work. When we are dealt a blow, or a series of blows, we grasp at straws and hold on for dear life to anything that brings an ounce of comfort. I held on to the idea of my angels. And from that day on, I've had a growing interest, almost obsession, with angels of any shape or size.

More than anything else, the practical problems centre around the simple absence of the partner after death. Just the fact that Bill was no longer with me seemed to double the difficulty of everything that had to be done. How to get tasks done at the bank or with taxes, and how to learn new skills can all be learned eventually, at any stage of life, I believe. What makes everything so much harder is having to do things on one's own, without the support, encouragement and wisdom of the person we chose to be with for life. Of course, family and friends help, but that is not the same as the comfort and counsel of a spouse. Being alone, after the companionship of marriage for many years, is such a disorientating break from "normality" that I think we lose confidence in our own abilities to cope with the practical side of life.

Coping – paying bills on time, putting out garbage on the right day, shovelling snow, dealing with contractors and professionals – all become small victories in our fight to rebuild self-confidence in the fabric of our lives. Knowing when to call a plumber, electrician, or any professional for minor repair, can be daunting. For the uninitiated, the difficulty is in not knowing whether or not a problem is minor and fixable, or major and requiring an expensive professional. Fortunately, I've been blessed in having friends to call on for advice. But I've always hesitated to ask for help, knowing they all have busy lives.

Reaching Out

The next couple of years were also difficult as I fought through panic attacks and bouts of anxiety. Worry about Steven was in the forefront of my mind. His anger, and subsequent behaviour towards other family members, was sometimes difficult to bare. And often I bore the brunt of everything that was wrong in his world. Looking back, it saddens me now to realize that although I did the best I could for my son, I was unable to provide him with what he needed to help him move forward on his own journey of grief. He was so angry, and not ready or willing to listen to anyone. I could understand, but often I wasn't much help in offering advice. More to the point, he did not want it. I also had tears enough of my own.

For a start, Steven didn't have the same support. At least my friends didn't turn their backs on me as I struggled to get through each day. I didn't have to go to work each day unprepared. Steven started working for Pepsi before his dad died and he continued working there until the summer of 2006.

I remember him arriving home distraught because he hadn't been able to see through his tears to sweep the floor. There were occasions when his penned-in emotions overwhelmed him and he had to leave work early because of it. This only resulted in black marks against him. Few people knew his pain.

I know now that I did not always give Steven credit for everything he did at the time of Bill and Richard's deaths. Perhaps numbed by my own pain, I wasn't always aware of the quiet help he was giving in spite of his own shock and grief. It was Steven who made the drive to Belleville with our friend Bob to tell Bill's parents of his death. It was Steven who again drove to Belleville to tell them of their grandson's death. (My friends delivered the news to my parents, always the morning after.) And it was Steven who made the funeral arrangements for his brother. I guess I wasn't able. Again, Steven made the trip to Belleville to pick up Nana on her own to attend Richard's funeral. Grandpa just wasn't able, so stayed home with a nurse. All these responsibilities took much courage, and Steven stepped up to the plate.

A grief victim tries hard to hide the tears. A survivor never leaves home without Kleenex. How wonderful it feels to give in and let tears flow when we are overwhelmed with emotions. Tears come from the soul, from our well of feelings rising from deep down. When we give in to the prickling behind our eyes and the lump in our throat to let teardrops fall from our eyes, we allow our feelings to surface so they can be set free.

Men don't discuss the pain of grieving. Common in every society are attitudes concerning acceptable behaviour for both men and women. No matter how often we hear about equality between the sexes, our expectations concerning how men and women react to situations remain unchanged, dictated by the society in which we were raised.

Males are expected to accept difficulties in their lives with a certain non-emotional response. In our culture, we equate being strong with repressing feelings. Women on the other hand are expected to cry, to fall apart at times, and to otherwise express their pain openly. The truth is that people experience emotional trauma in fairly predictable patterns regardless of gender but may express it differently. Research tells us clearly that men and women equally share 'feelings' of pain and grief. It is only in the methods one uses to deal with grief that the different responses become obvious.

The last thing most of us want to hear or think about when we are dealing with profound feelings of sadness is that deep learning can be found in this place. In the midst of our pain, we often feel picked on by life, or overwhelmed by the enormity of our loss. We may feel far too disappointed and angry to look for anything resembling a bright side to our suffering.

With courage, we can allow ourselves to cycle through the grieving process with full inner permission to experience it. This is a powerful teaching that sadness has to offer us. The ability to surrender and the acceptance of change go hand in hand. Sadness is something we all go through, and we all learn from it and are deepened by its presence in our lives. While our own individual experiences of sadness carry with them unique lessons, the implications of what we learn are universal. I have learned that the more we resist something, the longer it persists. There is no shame in letting tears flow freely and frequently. Tears are as natural to us as is breathing. When we honour our pain, we do just the opposite of resisting it, and as a result, we create a world in which we can own the fullness of what life has to offer.

Steven was far more isolated in his loss and grief. The fear of losing control in front of others or appearing weak kept him from openly discussing his loss. By repressing these feelings of sadness, he was using a great deal of energy, and therefore unable to move forward with his life. So often we felt he was living a life of diminished potential.

Steven is a hard worker, and honest to a fault, which would backfire on him later. As if he needed more worries…it was all so senseless. I was getting it out at grief counselling; he just wasn't ready for this. I hope that Steven will be able to find ways to loosen the bonds that tie him to the past. Only then, after colossal effort, will he be able to see himself as a valuable, productive and whole person again.

Unfortunately, there weren't men in our family who would come forward to help or include my son. Not having brothers or sisters, of course, there were no aunts or uncles to take him under their wing. After the deaths of his father and his brother, Steven lost a lot of friends; I assume because they just didn't know what to say to him and felt too uncomfortable with themselves to be with him.

Being a young man of 23, but without the same support that was available to me, must have been very difficult. Young people aren't equipped to deal with the emotional upheaval of tragedy. Dulling the pain with another beer or smoking pot seemed more appropriate than actually facing the reality of death, abandonment, loneliness and unimaginable emotional, physical and mental pain. And so, Steven's grief journey also began, yet one that was to be very different from mine.

As I write this, a light bulb has lit up in my mind. It's no wonder my son stayed away from so many family and other social gatherings. Avoidance is the key word. Why put yourself into a social situation when you foresee a breakdown? Time after time, one disappointment followed another for me. At every opportunity, I hoped he would join in, but he just wasn't able. Too often I was making excuses for his absence. Most men don't like to make themselves vulnerable. They know they can't handle it, so they stay away. Steven did that for years. Staying away from family and other social gatherings, from memorial services, or anything that would warrant keeping a stiff upper lip. It was easier to just avoid, much to my disappointment at the time. Now I understand. But if I could face challenging social situations, why couldn't he? Perhaps the answer has nothing at all to do with gender but is all about the person we are at the moment tragedy strikes us.

Through the grief work with counsellors that I have done, I've learned and experienced for myself that we may handle inconsolable grief in one of two ways – as grief victim or as grief survivor. Neither is a fixed position. Often we wobble between these two, depending on circumstances and the mileposts along our own path of tears. A grief victim gets caught in isolation. A survivor reaches out when she or he needs to. At times, a grief victim tries to block out memories. A grief survivor embraces memories of all kinds. Now I know we all have our different paths in our grief journey. I shouldn't have been so quick to judge. For a long time, Steven simply wasn't ready to reach out.

Challenges

One month after my father-in-law's death, I had another significant dream. It came after finally hearing from our family doctor, who did not call for three months after the deaths of my husband, son and father-in-law. This had been terribly upsetting and difficult for my family to understand, and I let him know under no uncertain terms.

My dream took place on a cruise ship. My mom, dad, and my dad's family were there. The main feature of the dream was the appearance of the doctor, after being conspicuously absent for so long. He presented me with two pairs of expensive, stress-releasing sunglasses. They were a very expensive peace offering and, after being disappointed and angry with him for what felt like his indifference, I was comforted he did this for me. It was like an apology. At that time, I felt closure because his gift allowed me to let go of my anger towards him. I understood that perhaps he didn't call right away because he simply didn't know what to say. Maybe he was giving me time to grieve. Whatever the case, I took the incident in the dream as a message from a Higher Power, maybe my angels, to forgive and to move on.

The doctor that attended to my husband after he died became my new doctor. It would be many years before Steven saw a doctor again. His doctor certainly wasn't calling him, although follow up would have been beneficial, as Steven was floundering in his grief. I must keep in mind however, that the patient is responsible for their own health, and at the time, perhaps Steven wasn't capable of caring enough to seek the help he needed. It was me who wanted it for him. When the doctor and Steven did connect, I felt the doctor wasn't seeing the whole picture in order to focus on what was necessary to keep my son under his care. But perhaps it was just time that was needed; time for Steven to be ready.

What began as a very pleasant afternoon and evening with a friend and his family ended in overwhelming despair for Steven. Social drinking before and after dinner, then reminiscing about what once was and never would be again was mentally and physically disabling on top of tiredness late at night. He planned to spend the night there, as suggested by his friend's Dad, but then thought he needed to be home in his own bed.

Uncontrollable grief has a knack of robbing you from common sense and logical thinking and/or decision making. This is when things can go wrong, as it did for Steven.

He attempted to make the short drive home but was picked up by police. I was called to the police station at 4:00 a.m. Barely being able to get by using my own coping skills, this only served to further complicate matters, not only for Steven, but also for myself. He was angry and belligerent. When it hurts so bad, with no one to ask and no window to go to, you vent that on the people closest to you. Disrespect comes into play, and especially when substance abuse plays a part. Then the side effects of the coping mechanism aren't good. I was on the receiving end, and at a loss to find a solution.

The end result of this mishap was loss of licence, company vehicle and job. A very hard lesson. Now what? Blame and more anger for him and more concern and worry for me. I wish that his friend's Dad had taken his keys from him. As they say, hindsight is 20/20.

Despite all these bumps in the road, there is a fight and desire to move forward, but the burden financially will take time to overcome. After losing a drivers licence for drinking and driving, one must take a back-on-track course, $500; install a breathalyzer, $1,000; not to mention the cost of the fine, and then car insurance, which may not be feasible to even consider for a while, at least not til he can afford to buy the car. Few were aware of the upheaval and devastation this mistake caused. If ever there can be a positive side, these adversities make us stronger and wiser. It might just take a while.

In life, there will always be times when we are adversely affected by the actions of others. This can be overwhelming and unproductive if it throws us off balance. When we are feeling criticized or attacked, it becomes very difficult to recover ourselves so that we can continue to speak and act our truth.

When we are the target of projections, as they are called in psychological terms, it can be confusing and frustrating, not to mention maddening, particularly when we know that we are not the cause of another person's distress.

I got to know a few grief counsellors. I had a favourite, and I was sorry when she retired. Another one I saw gave mixed messages and focused a lot on trying to push her religion. I felt her approach was wrong and some visits were distressing. It was time for me to make a change.

There comes a time in all our lives when we may need to evaluate our relationships, making sure that they are having a positive effect on us, rather than dragging us down. While we can try to avoid people we know who engage in projecting their "stuff" onto others, we can't always steer clear of such encounters. Without realizing it, we may be spending precious time and energy engaging in friendships that let us down, rather than cultivating ones that support and nourish us along our path. Life, with its many twists, turns and challenges is difficult enough without us entertaining people in our inner circle who drain our energy. I have learned that we can do so much more in this world when we are surrounded by people who understand what we're trying to do and who positively support our efforts to walk our path.

This is when we would do well to remember the old saying about letting certain things roll off us, like water off a duck's back. Sometimes however, when our lives are flooded with challenges, grief and pain, we may be tempted to believe that some individuals or incidents are simply bad or being vindictive. Most of the time, the attacks and criticisms of others have much more to do with them and how they are feeling than with us. If we get caught up in trying to adjust ourselves to other people's negative energy, we lose touch with our core. In fact, in a positive light, these slings and arrows offer us the opportunity to strengthen our core sense of self, and to learn to dodge and deflect other people's misdirected negativity. The more we do this, the more we are able to discern what belongs to us and what belongs to other people. With practice, we become masters of our energetic integrity, refusing to serve as targets for the disowned anger and frustration of the people around us. And so, I have learned that if we can allow the negativity to fade away, it is soon replaced by sympathetic tolerance. With each new challenge, we can learn to show great patience in the face of provocation and difficulties.

Ten years later, I was able to apologize to the doctor for my harsh words. He thanked me. I told him that I now understand that at the time of the deaths of my husband and son so close together, he may not have known what to say. He replied "I still don't!"

Significant holidays are a huge hurdle that we must encounter after a death in the family. And, if this isn't difficult enough to overcome, we have the added challenge of dealing with friends who think they know what's best for us. Their advice may be well meant, but often it only serves to heighten the anxiety we are already going through. Just the anticipation of an up-coming holiday can be daunting; though over the years, this can become a little less burdensome. Over time, and usually through trial and error, we learn personal strategies that help us get through these holidays, whether it be Easter, Christmas, anniversary days, birthdays, or other occasions that are particularly painful because of our loss. We have to honour our own needs and not be pressured into doing what feels uncomfortable.

Bill died in October, but Christmas was ahead and I had a need but not the energy to deal with gifts. Linda and Laurie to the rescue, wrapping every gift, ready to present on Christmas day. I even had a tree, laden with angels. I must confess it hasn't been up since.

Another challenge came when I realized it was time to replace my car. How could I do this without Bill? My Mom came with me; we were both naïve when it came to knowing the in's and out's of leasing a new vehicle. The process was a painful and difficult reminder of Bill's passing. We did it though, which was most pleasing with the help of a very accommodating staff at the Saturn dealership.

One friend of mine who lost a son did what was best for her family and herself by simply taking a holiday at Christmas time. Unfortunately, her sister didn't agree with this decision. Hard feelings ensued. Others don't always understand our grief. Sometimes we don't understand it ourselves, therefore making it difficult to help those who are struggling to understand and support us.

It wasn't long after Richard's death that, on occasion I was asked "Do you have children?" or "How many children do you have?" When I was in the company of friends, there was no fear of this. However, if they were strangers, there was always the possibility of that fearful question, and so the build up of tension was enormous. I needed a plan.

I thought about how I felt about my choices of answer and which one would most meet my needs. I had a surviving son, but to say "one" would seem a denial that my other son had lived, and that wasn't right for me. In the beginning, when I still needed to tell people that my son had died, I did so in detail. As time passed, so did my needs. The criteria I use in determining my answer is whether the person asking is going to be a continuing part in my life. If so, they need to know about my son, and I tell them. Better, I think, to have it out in the open. Otherwise, all that needs to be said is "I had two children." Seldom does anyone catch the "had" instead of "have", and pursue it. Although I still sometimes feel uncomfortable in these situations, particularly in the anticipation of the question, I am no longer quite as anxious about it as I was in the beginning.

The funeral home director that I dealt with took me to a location where I could choose a large rock for placement at the cemetery. The one that I chose was perfect with a suitable spot for the bronze plaque. It even had hens and chickens (perennial plant) growing out of it, which was an added bonus. When I asked how much, the proprietor said fifty dollars, plus ten dollars for him to put the plaque on. I agreed to this and said we would pick up the rock upon completion. The proprietor said "No trouble"…he was in Oakville all the time and he didn't mind delivering it. There was no mention of a shipping charge. I received the invoice in the mail for $97.75. The plaque had been placed incorrectly on the rock, meaning that it had to go in the ground with the plants no longer visible. It wasn't the same as I had seen it in his garden. I thought it was unfair of him to assume that we would know he really meant $75.00 when he said $50.00. I suggested that it would be to his advantage to be upfront with people, and explain his charges ahead of time, so that there are no surprises when the bill is received. I paid him $69.00 and moved on.

And so, my journey of healing continued. Always with many challenges along the way, sometimes overwhelming and often no fun. Sometimes I felt like I was standing at the corner of "walk" and "don't walk!"

I read many books on grieving and self-help that warned me of the downhill problems many people face when grieving after a tragedy. One danger was turning to alcohol to numb the pain. "Whatever you do, don't drink!" the authors said repeatedly. Fortunately for me, this was not a temptation as I've never been much of a drinker.

However, I did experience panic attacks that left me frightened and nauseous. My doctor prescribed an anxiety pill which helped to take the edge off my attacks. I stopped taking them after some time, and had withdrawal symptoms from quitting cold turkey. I suppose, at the time, I needed them but I would hate to be dependent on anything like that ever again. It seemed that nothing, absolutely nothing, could divert my thoughts from grief. For a long time, death and grief seemed to be all around me. For example, my Uncle Jim died on exactly the same day as my son and my Aunt Marion died on exactly the same day as my father-in-law. Of course, I wasn't able to attend their funerals. All the pockets of my mind, my heart and my soul became bloated with pain. The trouble with grief is that it is so internal and subjective, so much a part of us that it can't be viewed. I have tried to describe the experience of grief in many different ways; for example, like the waves of the ocean, lapping onto the shore, recessing into the sea, but always coming again, sometimes somewhat diminished, but never disappearing completely. This was Bill Brown's description of grief. He was our minister at the time.

Just as Bill used the analogy of the waves to describe grief, I have since learned that when we ride the wave of life, we can evolve naturally and with minimal effort. Because life is dynamic and always changing, it is when we try to make the wave stand still or resist its direction that we are likely to get pulled under by its weight.

Always the challenge was not only to remember Bill and Richard, and my other relatives, as they were when they were alive, but also to try to make some sort of sense of their deaths. Bill was in the prime of life. Children are not supposed to die before their parents. I wanted answers, or at least, to find comfort enough to be able to re-orientate myself in the world in which I and my other son, Steven were still living. The visits I received from Bill Brown were timely and helpful. He often came with a casserole from the church ladies, and his kind words were comforting. When he came the day after my son Richard's death, my aunt said to Bill Brown, "You're going to have a hard time explaining this one Bill!" At the funeral, the first thing he said was, "If I thought God was in any way responsible for this, I wouldn't be up here doing what I do." I always remember those words. I believe God has guided me through my healing journey. Otherwise, I question where my strength has come from. Perhaps my resilience comes from my mother. She was a very stoic woman, as was her mother. Our Scottish background may play a part, in that we are very independent, strong, reserved and often undemonstrative.

Many years ago, and long before I personally experienced death, my mom exclaimed, "Well, we can't live forever Enid!" This came after the demise of an acquaintance of hers, and I felt compassion, knowing her sadness. I don't know why I've never forgotten those words. I thought it was rather a profound statement, and one that, when put into perspective, allows acceptance of death. How true it is that we can't live forever. As crazy as it sounds, my mom's common sense has given me some comfort when I've come face to face with the reality of death. And I've shared her simple words with friends and have also heard them repeated. My mom's message is significant and comes through loud and clear.

One day, Barbara Underhill, 1984 World Pairs figure skating champion, came to visit me. She too had lost a child; one of her twin daughters, who drowned in their swimming pool on the day before the twins' christening. Even after seven years, the pain of her tragic loss was still very fresh. Barb had set up a foundation designed to educate people about child safety. She gave me a copy of a CD given to her by Amy Sky and the video of her final skating show with Paul Martini.

She also gave me a little Beanie Baby bear. His name is Hope. I winced as I opened the little heart-shaped birth card that came with the bear and read that Hope was born on March 23rd, the day after my son's death. A coincidence? I don't think so. Barb wished me courage, strength, and HOPE as I travelled this difficult journey. I was very touched by her kindness. I received my first pocket angel from Barb, which would bring comfort and inspiration with me wherever I went. When I needed extra courage, hope or reassurance, I could hold my angel in my palm and rub as I might rub a worry stone

Barbara invited my friend Diana and me to attend a Women of Excellence conference as her guests. She was a wonderful speaker, sharing not only the details of her loss, but also the little things that brought her comfort. For example, a lone forget-me-not appearing as the first sign of spring, burst through the cement on the pool deck on the first anniversary of her daughter's death. It had been a difficult task to even look through the pool gate, but on this occasion, the purple colour caught her eye. This was surely a sign that her daughter's spirit was still alive.

One evening, Barbara and I went to a Bereaved Families meeting together. I could see that she was still raw with pain, which eased when the guest speaker was introduced. He had lost a young son to a tornado while camping in Calgary. Barb had gone to high school with him, so their friendship was renewed that evening. They sure had something in common, i.e. the tragic loss of a child and the realization for both that we are never alone. There is always someone else who shares a similar pain. No one gets off scot-free. As my mom used to say, "Everyone has their own cross to bear."

Barb's new beginning came on the 10th year anniversary of her daughter's death. Their cat Boo was expecting babies, and the anticipation of them being born on the same date Stephanie died had been draining for Barb. The day came and went without kittens, but in the early hours of the next morning, Samantha, Stephanie's twin sister, shouted from her bedroom that Boo was delivering. Precisely at that moment, a heaviness that had lain over Barb like an unwelcome blanket was lifted. It was 1:11 a.m., the day after the 10th anniversary of Stephanie's death. Samantha suggested to her

Mom that this was Stephanie's plan…a new day, a new beginning. Sam said … "Mom, this is a message from Stephanie…she doesn't want us to be sad anymore; she wants us to be happy." Those words struck Barb like a lightening bolt, and from then on she was determined to let the sadness go…for Sam, Stephanie and their family. And so, Barb took comfort by believing her daughter's life-affirming message that she was okay. Barb could now move forward.

Time and again, living through grief has felt like being on a long journey. Indeed, I believe it is a journey that will never really end. And, like any journey, there are ups and downs, moments of peace, even happiness, and times of great pain and boredom. To feel sad endlessly is boring, but it is a stretch of countryside that one must pass through. Sometimes we seem to be stopped at a particular station of grief for a long time, then, almost unaccountably, our journey moves forward again.

More than a couple of years passed after the deaths of my husband, son and father-in-law. My mother-in-law was grappling with the prospect of selling her lovely home on the Bay of Quinte and moving to Oakville. She didn't want to be a burden and didn't expect me to travel to Belleville in the event of her becoming ill. Who was she kidding? Of course, I would want to be by her side, so we got the ball rolling towards her moving to Oakville. She had to sell many items to antique dealers and much went to the Salvation Army. A chance visit from an Oakville friend prompted a conversation about moving. Coincidentally, this friend wanted to buy precisely where my mother-in-law was moving from. And so, that Higher Power I spoke of earlier was hard at work directing Mary to us. She and her husband bought my mother-in-law's home. Then we packed up, locked the door and drove away, just the two of us, in tears. We realized the extent of our losses but, at that moment, we also recognized our choices. We could choose to wallow in sorrow or to pick up and move on. We decided then, we must "buck-up" for our men. This is what they would have wanted.

My mother-in-law settled into Oakville famously. My friends soon became her friends. At 89 years old in 2009, she still enjoys many pleasures and hobbies, living in the same condominium complex where my parents lived, just a short distance from my home. Our bond is strong and we're always helping each other. We cope as best we can with our new life.

A pleasure for both of us is working at the cemetery garden, a labour of love and constructive grief work. Even this came with challenge. To soften the look around the bench and tree, I added top soil and planted some perennials. The cemetery staff eliminated most of it, i.e. ferns, old English daisies, pachysandra and periwinkle ground cover. When I realized that they had been over zealous with the weed eater, I was very discouraged, and saw it as careless incompetence. I let them know. If they go in there with "blinders" on, as was suggested to me by the maintenance manager, it's time they took them off and did their job with respect, not to mention sensitivity and concern. Only a half-wit would not recognize that these were special plantings and not weeds. Of course, they felt very badly, and the student that was responsible introduced himself to me as "the half-wit". My letter of complaint had been posted in the office. We had a good laugh and all was forgotten.

Contrary to this, and coincidentally, my memorial garden has been maintained almost every year by someone who knew my family. As students, working for the town, their area was the cemetery, and so we were fortunate to have their loving attention. I was known as 'the resident gardener' by the cemetery staff.

Enid & Bill
Cheers!

Coping with S.T.U.G.

My grief counsellor talked a lot about triggers. Oh, there were so many! How the floodgates would open. I continued my dance classes on and off, and sometimes a piece of music would trigger a memory. I tried so hard to hold back the tears that at times my throat would hurt so much I felt like screaming, which wouldn't have been appropriate in the middle of a dance class. Letting the tears flow did feel better. At least I was always in good company.

I developed a sinus problem that concerned me enough to call the doctor. He referred me to a specialist and I had the usual "tubes down the nose" test. It appeared nothing was wrong. I diagnosed the problem myself as too much crying and I expected this discomfort to cease as the years passed. I was right. No more sinus problem.

Considering the stress and anxiety I was under, I was also walking around with my shoulders up to my ears, as if 'on guard' for the next blow. This resulted in much pain in my neck and upper body.

In time, and as I became aware of the unwanted tension I was creating, I was able to find physiotherapy and exercise to help me relax.

Despite my anguish at times, I often made an effort to attend social functions, even for a short while, usually in the company of supportive friends. Sometimes I forced myself to do things too soon and occasionally things backfired.

I will always remember a family 50th birthday celebration, just three months after Richard's death. It was in a fancy restaurant. Every guest was seated with a stranger, separated from their partner. Under normal circumstances, this would have been all right, but given my circumstances, I was far from being ready for this. No one at my table knew me, or knew why I left. It was a very embarrassing position to have to be in. Because I was separated from anyone I knew and so far out of my comfort zone, I had to leave even before dinner was served. Even that was difficult, knowing they were serving a favourite dish of sea bass. I wasn't able to go back. Unfortunately my quiet exit, far from disrupting the celebration, left the hostess with a grudge. She said, "Family ruined my birthday." Their feelings may have been hurt because I was unable to attend their party, but how could they know how utterly my life had been shattered by the deaths of my husband, son, father-in-law, aunt, uncle, and our Kipper who we so loved. No one has ever treated me like that again. And I became more cautious when deciding whether or not to attend functions, and whether or not I was emotionally ready. Another friend, on a separate occasion, but not too long after, told me how hurt she was that I didn't attend her birthday party. I had certainly called to let them know I wouldn't be coming. I often felt it was a 'no win' for me. Some friends were very understanding, others were not. Sometimes, people just said the wrong thing, though I believe their intentions were good.

Because I felt compassion, I attended other funerals much too soon. I made a presence, trying to show support to friends who had lost loved ones, but it was really too early for me after my own losses. In hindsight, it may have been better to show my respect in other ways, rather than trying to be present at the memorial service when I was so raw in my own grief.

It was during a yoga class, ten years later that I broke down, when a friend from the past walked in. Her son had played sports with Richard. It was many years since I had seen her. This had been a trigger I guess. I was happy in seeing her, but churned up memories opened up the floodgates, full tilt. How fortunate it was just a small class. The teacher stopped the class and embraced me while I cried out of control. They allowed me to feel my pain and I was very comforted and touched by their kindness and compassion.

I've received much advice to sell my house and move on. I am preparing to do so, but the process of letting go is slow. One of Bill's hobbies was stained glass and as a result, I feel blessed to be surrounded by his beautiful work in my home. His projects were large, i.e. French doors, and the side panels at my front door. It has been suggested to me that I should leave them behind and move on. Easy for them to say! How would they feel I wonder, if it were their husband's fine work? Maybe not so willing to part with such a treasure. I've had to take a lot of advice from friends, though well-intentioned, with a grain of salt and follow my own heart instead. Only we, who are without our loved ones, know when the time is right to part with certain things. No one can dictate to us about something that is so personal.

That being said, going through my husband's and my son's belongings was no easy task. I did do it very methodically, giving lots of thought to who should be the recipients of their treasures.

A friend who lost her husband was devastated after his family came and removed all his belongings. It happened so quickly, before she was ready. She was, however, able to hang on to his camera, which they asked for, but she felt badly about not handing that over too. Or, did they put pressure on her to give it up? Whatever the case, she was left with hard feelings.

For myself, I am only now, after all these years, able to look through the dozens of boxes of slide carousels, old pictures and so many memories. Some I will save, others have to go, along with the projectors which are now outdated. For someone, it will be a treasure they will be happy to take off my hands. All this takes much time.

I have agonized over some things friends have said or done, and sometimes I've been angry with myself for being too sensitive. Why can't I just shrug it off? Then, after talking about it, the unnecessary tension caused by dwelling on negativity fades away and is replaced by that sympathetic tolerance I spoke of earlier. I remind myself that there are no real targets in an emotional attack and that it is usually a way for the attacker to redirect their uncomfortable feelings away from themselves. People who are overcome with their own strong emotions often see themselves as victims and lash out at others as a means of protection and to make themselves feel better. Easy as it is to criticize people and situations when they frustrate or hurt us, we do ourselves a disservice in the process. Instead of being tempted to believe that some individuals or incidents are simply bad, I now treat each new challenge as another chance to prove myself by showing great patience in the face of difficulty.

Even so, I did have some disappointments. I had to give up Sorority, an International woman's organization I had belonged to for over 20 years. Every time we had a guest to a meeting, each of us had to introduce and tell a little about ourselves. For me the emotional tension was overbearing. Every time it was my turn to speak, my floodgates would open because, to me, my truth was unspeakable.

My grief counsellor had a name for the unpredictable incidents. S.T.U.G., which stands for Sudden Temporary Upsurge of Grief. All of a sudden, my unwelcome experiences had a name. It was normal, and now I understood what was happening. Somehow, it made them easier to go through it.

I did attend one bereavement group for people who had experienced the loss of a child. But I fell apart at that meeting too…everyone was with their spouse. My husband wasn't there for support. Everyone had a story. One couple had just lost their youngster when she was run over by the school bus she just got off. The wind took her drawing from her little hand and she ran to retrieve it in front of the stopped bus. The bus pulled ahead as the parents watched in horror. I left the meeting and cried all the way home. I never went back to that particular group and probably should not have gone in the first place.

In November of 2004, the Common Cup Company was the highlight at church. They were a musical performance group of which our Interim Minister was a part. I had the pleasure of performing with them at our LAFF (community outreach) event. I sang Marriage Vine with the orchestra. This was good practice, as I would be singing it soon at a wedding.

While the Common Cup Company were in town, they conducted a song-writing workshop at our church. I was excited about this and looking forward to getting helpful input about my own songs – about life experiences, losses, and moving forward. One of the men running the workshop was a bishop; another was a minister who proceeded with a prayer in order to get us motivated. To start us off, we were given the phrase, "It's a pleasant place". I closed my eyes and tried to find happy words, but couldn't. I immediately thought, "He said it's a pleasant place, so why do I feel pain? Why can't I find the place he speaks of? I'm trying to put on a good front, but the journey seems so long, as if it will never end." All of a sudden I felt overcome with grief. My floodgates opened.

I felt too upset to continue with the workshop. But when, with difficulty, I spoke to the bishop, his words were comforting and I was able to settle down. At that moment, Gord, the gentleman from the funeral home I had been dealing with for four funerals, walked in with a floral arrangement for the Sunday service. What unusual timing this was, I thought. Gord was so connected with my grief history, considering all I had been through with him. He had even taken me in search of a special rock to serve as a marker at the cemetery.

I did go back into the room to finish the workshop, but still found it very difficult. We are never alone in our grief and my sadness brought to the surface other sadness's in the room. Two people asked me to stay afterwards so that they could talk to me. He was a retired professor at Windsor University and she was a music ministry leader and song writer. Together they were publishing a book of poetry. They were very interesting to talk to and she gave me her CD, "Come to my Heart: Touching the Spirit". I stayed connected with these two people, and they came as guest speakers at a subsequent LAFF (Life After Fifty-Five) event, for which I am Programme Co-ordinator.

Though I didn't come away from the workshop with a song, I did gain a life experience. The next day at church, the Minister said, "For those of us who have a song to sing but can't sing it, Lord Hear Our Prayer." Another God-incidence? I'm sure the reference was made towards me. Perhaps it wasn't a song I was to write, but rather a book, which I have since been able to follow through to completion.

So I move on. Anguish still surfaces. And grief sneaks up to ambush me when I'm unprepared. Recently Jeff, our church minister, caught my attention when he said that grief has no time limit. "It is woven in us and through us," he said. How true! Always, there are reminders of the people I loved so much – a car like the one Bill drove, a familiar tune, a turnip in a supermarket, one of the few vegetables my husband enjoyed. When I go to the rink and see hockey in progress, or kids on the street playing basketball, or a Young Drivers vehicle. So many triggers still have the power to overwhelm me, but I'm not afraid of them anymore. Now I understand they are so powerful precisely because they remind me of the people I loved. I like to be reminded of them. I loved them dearly and that is why I hurt so much. I'm very touched if someone tells me they've been to the cemetery and memorial garden to visit my loved ones. They are remembering, and this gives me much comfort.

On My Skates Again

Time passes. Life does not return to normal, but what we like to call 'reality' has a way of including us once again. As the months passed after the death of my son Richard, I had to face a new challenge if I wanted to continue my job as a skating instructor. I love skating; I love the sense of freedom of being out on the ice, the grace of movement and its physical demands. If I wanted to continue coaching young people to also find this joy for themselves, I knew I would have to go back to the rink where my son died. How could I ever step foot on that ice again?

During the summer school at which my friend Ann was teaching, she invited me to come to the rink, don my skates once more and re-live the horrible night when Richard collapsed and died on the ice. She would be there to support me. I hoped that after a few times on the ice with no pressure or commitment to teach, I would be ready to take on the onslaught of keen learn-to-skaters in the fall session. "Just like getting back up on a horse after a fall," I told myself. I couldn't help feeling apprehensive. Ann's presence was a comfort, and on one of these occasions, my mom and aunt came with me to the rink as Olympian Elvis Stojko was going to be on the ice, working with some competitive skaters in our Club. It was rather a thrill to be on the ice with him. There were some emotional moments, but in the end I found going out on the ice easier than I'd expected. This was probably because, after all the emotional turmoil of Bill and Richard's deaths, I was returning to an activity I have always loved and continue to love.

However, major changes were taking place regarding my job as a skating instructor. I had been working for the Town of Oakville (now a city with a population over 160,000). In any event, all the recreational skating programs were being taken over by the skating club, which meant it would come under the umbrella of the governing body for figure skating in Canada. In order to continue coaching, it was mandatory that I become certified. I signed up for the course but could see that timing would be a problem because of my mom's failing health, which brought added pressure and required many visits to her in the hospital. At the same time I was looking after my elderly dad, who was on his own in their condo. In August, I explained my situation, hoping for an extension, so that I would be able to teach in the Fall. But the bureaucracy of the governing body had set a firm deadline and wouldn't budge. I was devastated. My family was dead and dying and now I was going to lose my job as well. Again, my angels rallied. The Board of Directors at the skating club cleared the way for me to complete the course requirements on a one-to-one basis when more convenient, and this allowed me to become certified and able to teach the upcoming fall session.

As a skating coach, it is imperative to update emergency first aid knowledge every couple of years. In doing so, hands-on CPR training is part of the course. My grief came to the fore when it was time to practice on the CPR dummy. My focus was only that it hadn't worked for my loved ones. The course leader gave me permission to leave the room if and when I felt overwhelmed. I can truthfully say that I was indeed overwhelmed the first time. Thankfully I need only to do this every few years.

Angels, dreams, and visions – I welcomed them all if they eased the burden of pain and helped me to come to terms with what had happened.

In August 2004, I made another trip to Vernon, British Columbia, where my friend Andrea took me to see Ashleigh, a spiritualist, in whom she put a lot of trust. I was sceptical. However, after the reading, I came away with many things to think about.

Ashleigh detected that I was walking about with a hatchet in my back, and that I was also constantly hitting myself against a wall, a barrier stopping me from moving forward. She thought these two "obstacles" were caused by grief. I had never met Ashleigh before. She knew nothing about me. A blue bird was significant; also, "Little Boy Blue".

She told me that a young man, and corrected herself to say an older boy, was standing beside me, telling me that he was okay, with lots of things to do. "I'm here Mommy!" he was saying. He promised he would be here for me. All I needed to do was to ask for him.

Ashleigh said an older woman was sitting beside me. She asked if my mom had passed. I told her "Yes". She asked if she was Scottish. "Did she speak her mind?" Ashleigh asked. I felt a connection. Ashleigh certainly said things that convinced me she was in touch with the spirit world. I was very moved.

I went with a group of church friends to visit a full spectrum psychic with the gifts of Clairvoyance (seeing the future) and Clairsentience (physical sensing of energy). Here, we were to explore and understand our present life circumstances to assist in enlightening and empowering us to create our best future. She used Zen Tarot Cards, and the first two drawn for me were 'Healing' and 'Guidance'. I thought, how coincidental, as I most certainly needed both. She said I must reassess my obligation to others and start looking after myself. She said "Start honouring yourself and feel your pain." I don't know how she even knew that I was in pain. We were at a Tea Room, enjoying a lovely lunch.

That being said, I lost some sleep over a friend's concern for me that I would even consider visiting such a person. She insisted I ask the Lord for forgiveness; anyone of this nature is from the devil and she provided the scripture readings from the

Bible to prove her facts. I wondered how anything that brought me comfort could be so bad. I resolved this dilemma by seeking the advice of three ministers. They all gave me their blessing and permission to enjoy the gift of anyone who is able to provide messages from the spirit world. One said that it also says in the Bible that all women must cut their hair and not speak. Do we follow those same rules today? Of course not. Fundamentalist thinking is of this vain and not mine.

Cemetery arrangements are just one of the many things to think about after a death. Whatever was decided had to be just right and sometimes this was difficult to decide. Yet, as each quandary arose, and I was tortured with confusion not knowing what to do, a solution would fall from the sky, or so it seemed. One of these occasions was when I was contemplating whether or not to purchase a memorial bench to place in the cemetery.

In the book, "Talking to Heaven", the section on dreams says that the easiest way to reach spirits in the sleep state is to think about them before falling asleep. For me that wasn't difficult. They were my constant focus. One night, in the midst of my confusion over the bench, my husband came to me in a dream. We were sitting together on a bench; hence, I was sure I was receiving Bill's approval to go ahead and purchase the bench for the cemetery.

There was one more dream that I've saved until now. I have spoken of this only once before, in a Bible class when Rev. Bill Brown asked if anyone had felt God's presence. I told my story. I was in bed, fully awake, when I saw before me, all in white, a vision of Jesus with a young man close behind him. I tried to speak but couldn't. I was frozen stiff at seeing what was before me. The vision left as quickly as it came, and this left me feeling paralyzed until daylight, when I called my mom. Could this possibly have been a visit? Was this a message that Richard was safely in God's hands? I liked to believe that it was. Some felt strongly that I was very blessed to have had such a visit. This very intimate experience has not been something I've wanted to share with everyone before now. Whatever the truth, it has brought me some comfort, and for that I am grateful. I see it now as an important part of the process, the journey of grieving.

The night before I had been at a friend's, looking at her photographs of the Passion Play at Oberammergau in Germany. Of course, there were lots of pictures of Jesus, so this was fresh on my mind. However, I prefer to believe that my vision was real, because I felt to be just as awake then as I am now while writing these words.

When I told my friend Pat what had happened she asked me if I knew how lucky I was. She said that at a time when I was so fragile, the Lord was sending me inner locutions. "He's finding ways to give you strength to be a 'survivor'," she said. She reminded me of the story of the "Footsteps in the Sand", another analogy of how Jesus was carrying me through my darkness by giving me a vision. "You're blessed right out of your socks!" Pat told me.

It seems to me that when I share a story, I hear of another that has somehow touched someone's life, or at least brought to them a realization of deeper truths.

As my friend mourned the loss of his son after a tragic car accident, he stood in his garden and asked God for a sign that his boy was with him. Not only did he get a sign, but the day it came was significant. A wild red poppy in their garden on Remembrance Day, November 11th. The enormity of the significance of the red poppy was of course that it is a symbol of remembrance, but even more so that their son was born on the same day. The one poppy that arrived that day has now turned to over 2000 poppies, three years later. A field of red, and only on their property, with not a single one blowing over to their neighbours right next to them.

Then there's Michael, who passed into the mystery of death, after his plane crashed. He wore a family signet ring that had been in need of repair. His mom was to have taken it to the jewellers but had forgotten to get it from him when she saw him last. After Michael's death, his mom and sister paid a visit to a spiritual consultant. There was a message for them. "Someone is glad that he forgot to give you the ring." That was a clear and precise message that Michael's spirit was there with them. No doubt they came away from there feeling somewhat comforted. What a powerful gift it must be to be able to be in touch with the spirit world. People of this nature are often approached by the police to solve major crimes. For those of us whose loved ones have gone before us, it gives a feeling of connectedness. Just when we think all is lost, we are reminded that perhaps there is more to know or imagine about the mystery of death and what lies thereafter.

I too paid a visit to this consultant, who clearly received energies from my loved ones. She asked me "Where's the Dick connection?" This was my father's name. I seem to be surrounded in papers and my husband is at my back and very proud of me. I took this as a reference to "Soldier On" and the stacks of papers around me. She also knew dates and precisely the number of years that my loved ones have been gone. She acknowledged they were very much okay and very organized on the other side. Richard was a strong spokesperson for them all, with a particular focus on Steve, his big brother.

I love the saying "Just when the caterpillar thought the world was over, it became a butterfly."

Meanwhile, my son Steven's struggles were beyond my control at this point. He was living in a not-so-ideal environment. Unhappy with his job, angry at the world - and I was always bearing the brunt of it. He wouldn't consider counselling at this point. A grief victim fears the moments of grief. A survivor welcomes those moments. Steven wasn't ready. He was attempting to hold all his pain inside himself, yet his grief was overflowing and the dam was just waiting to burst. If only he would allow it. A typical answer, when asked how he was doing was, "I'm fine." Of course, now I know that F.I.N.E. really stands for "feelings inside not expressed."

Steven and Richard
"Adoration"

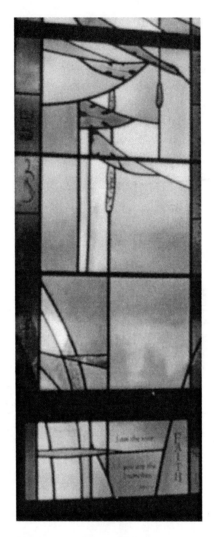

FAITH . . . I am the vine,
you are the branches

John 15

Deaths of My Parents

For most of us, a natural part of the cycle of life is when our roles as children start to shift from that into caretaking roles where our parents are concerned. Such a shift is momentous as it signals a time of confronting our own mortality as we confront that of our parents. My parents cared well for me when I was young. Now it was my turn, and I found myself consumed with fear at the thought of losing them too.

I had wonderful parents, with whom I was very close. I was their only child. (They had lost their first baby from meningitis at three weeks old.) In 2001, my mom was suffering with fractured vertebrae. She hadn't fallen, but a combination of C.O.P.D. (chronic obstructive pulmonary disorder), bouts of coughing and osteoporosis may have been the cause. Her coughing was laboured because of the pain and so she ended up with pneumonia and had to be in hospital for three months. Her stay was not a happy one. During my frequent visits I often felt that she was a victim, not the patient. It was heartbreaking to watch a loved one deteriorate because of the so-called "system".

So many mistakes seemed to be made and there seemed such a consistent pattern of sloppiness at the hospital that I wrote a 6-page report and sent it to management at the hospital. It also went to the Minister of Health, the Mayor, the local MPP, and the president of the Hospital Association. Most replied to say they appreciated the information and had forwarded my letter directly to a senior official at the hospital. Every one of them passed the buck! It seemed that no one wanted to take on resolving the issues. It was out of sheer anguish, frustration and lack of energy to fight any longer, that I began writing a daily journal in order to maintain my sanity. We felt we were wasting our breath after endless exasperating incidents that left us feeling powerless and weak. When feeling a need to express concerns to nurses, doctors, or anyone else who would listen, there was no doubt that feelings were mutual; but often the response was defensive.

I was in touch with the hospital ombudsman, from whom I received an apology and a promise to attempt to change many of their systems by using my issues and concerns to help bring this about.

On one occasion, my mom's sister had a heart attack at the nurse's station. She had followed the nurse out of my mom's room, reprimanding her for a demeaning remark that she had made with regards to my mom's health. We were truly at the end of our rope and could no longer stay quiet. Of course, my aunt was admitted.

At the same time, my mother-in-law was in the same hospital with complications after a hysterectomy. All three were on the fourth floor of the hospital. I did a lot of room hopping and also visiting my dad in their condo who, because of dementia, was confused about where my mom was. He would make her porridge for breakfast, and wonder why it was untouched. Despite our many hospital visits to see her, it seemed he was in denial about her ill-health. It didn't take long before all these emotional demands overwhelmed me. At this time, I found myself in a further state of anxiety, trying to protect my Mom from knowing about the devastation of 9/11, September of 2001. This would have upset her greatly, as it did us all. Steven was on his own journey, not offering, and perhaps not able to assist.

Because of time constraints, work load and shortage of nursing staff, there was no time for proper patient care. My concern about a foul smell in my Mom's room went unaddressed for days. I finally discovered on my own that it was rotting flesh from open and infected bed sores. This was sickening and deplorable that it happened in the first place. Their solution? ... a little paper cup filled with peppermint oil on the bedside table. End result? ... oil on the floor, which my Mom slipped on and fell. How did I find out? From the roommate; the bed rail had not been put up. Just writing this makes me tearful and of course, angry. The incidents were many, relating to medications, patient transfer, communication, standard of care and staff education. What we experienced was an absolute lack of professionalism, and any answers that were weak, pathetic, and lacking any sense of anger at the crass stupidity and lack of sensitivity or interest did not carry any weight with my family. The hospital slogan "Caring for Today, Growing for Tomorrow" in my opinion is a travesty and mockery, which reflects on the management, who, for the most part, did not listen to us. My Mom's needs were not addressed and what transpired was inexcusable. As I told the ombudsman, the horror of our experience still lingers. It was a social worker who strongly suggested I speak out and voice my concerns, which she felt were so valid.

Thankfully, my cousin Margaret arrived from Seattle to help. She had just returned home to Seattle from Toronto, where she'd been assisting her own elderly dad. She called and offered to come right back and nurse my mom. She said she'd thought deeply about this on her flight home and that she was sure she wanted to help. I felt very blessed to have her kindness and assistance during this difficult time. She was a Godsend. It was easy to write a poem about her when asked for something to include in a memory book that her friend was making as a surprise for Margaret's 50th birthday.

Margaret is my cousin
Of this I'm very proud
I'd rather be her sister
If it were allowed
She has two other sisters
Does she really need one more?
If she would consider
The prospect, I'd adore
But cousins, twice removed we are
And living far apart
But matter not it doesn't
When it comes to gifts from heart
For you see, our Margaret
Is a lass I truly love
Her kindness, warmth and outreach
Is over and above
She has a special way
That warms the hearts of all
A caring nurse, a loving wife;
The consensus...she's a doll
Margaret was an angel
Who gave so of her time
To nurse my Mom so willingly
And to keep things so in line
The help I was in need of
And she so quickly came
After flying home
Then flying back again
Now, who else would do this
But a kindly soul as she
If I can't be her sister,
A proud cousin I will be

My mom passed away in September of 2001. My Uncle Stuart, a retired minister and Margaret's father, conducted her funeral service, along with Bill Brown, our minister. (Uncle Stuart had already done the service for my husband, but he was away when Richard died.) Then Uncle Stuart died. I sang at his funeral. (His wife Marion had died on exactly the same day as my father-in-law.) I breezed through my mom's funeral and gave her eulogy. It appeared as if I was in control of my life, that I was taking everything in my stride. I had no tears left for crying. My friends were telling me I wasn't myself, that I was acting like a robot, attending to every detail, but capable of doing so only by taking pills to suppress anxiety. (I no longer take them.) I wasn't aware of the strain I was under; that it was all too much. Too many deaths (six people gone in five months) and now my own mother. Too many funerals. Too many thank you notes to write, on top of looking after my mom's finances and selling my parent's home.

It was around this time that I was devastated, along with most others in our congregation, to learn that Bill Brown, our minister, and his assistant were leaving our church. Another blow. This one came as a real shock. I wept in disbelief as I sat in the pew. I was not alone. Most of my church family were in shock at hearing this news. There was little explanation, and it was impossible for most of us to imagine that our church would ever be whole again. Bill Brown was so loved, and would be much missed. He had been a great support to me. We were angry and very sad.

Another loss. His working partner, our secondary minister, resigned at the same time, all in all, a terrible upset.

After all the deaths, anger, trials and difficulties, it seemed that I needed another focus. This came when I received in the mail a survey from Statistics Canada collecting information about our health, well-being and our use of health care services. I thought this was timely, since I had so much to say after my personal experiences. They wanted information and I was ready to give it. My thoughts? Maybe I could be instrumental in helping to change our health care system! I had a story all right. I gave them an earful. Surprisingly, they contacted me directly, requesting more information. The LHIN (Local Health Integration Network) was formed "to initiate discussions with local hospitals and Community Care Access Centres, to ensure that the health system continues to put a priority on good client service and responsiveness, and to develop a process for communicating consumer concerns to the LHIN on issues within their mandate." I don't know of anyone who has been a recipient of good client service and responsiveness. According to friends who work at the hospital, there have been no changes. This subject angers me every time I recall the treatment and lack of care my family received at the hospital.

In the meantime, my dad was confused with dementia. At 86, he too needed my assistance. As I was pulling out after visiting my Dad, the condominium security guard told me in a very caring way that my Dad had been outside in his pajamas at 3:00 in the morning. I just wept. I was grateful for his assistance in getting my Dad back to his apartment. When I wasn't crying, I was laughing, especially when my Dad told me he had been over to the local bakery at 6:00 in the morning, asking them for a job.

I made arrangements to sell the condo and he moved into a retirement home, where he was as happy and well settled as could be expected. This move was another huge undertaking. More packing and selling of treasures. My involvement at the retirement home, as a volunteer, took much of my time but I enjoyed being with the seniors, and, of course, spending time with my dad. We were very close. He called me his angel. I couldn't do enough for this sweet, gentle man. Love, care and protection were first and foremost, even when he called me in the middle of the night. I had set up his phone so that he needed only to press #1 to reach me. I was often tired, but if I was able to settle and comfort my dad, I was happy. Sometimes, he would have a wee cry when I had to remind him that mommy was dead. In his mind, she was just out shopping; a very comforting thought.

Life went on with continued visits and outings with my dad and the odd upset at the retirement home. One day, they made a big mistake, for which no one would take responsibility. They administered a drug in error to him that really upset his demeanour. I'm sure that things like this happen a lot more than what we hear about. Then they had the nerve to call and complain to me about his behaviour. One nurse eventually apologized to me, but not before I had taken them to task for what seemed like their uninterest. They may have thought I was entitled to sue, but that wasn't my intention. What I needed was for them to care enough to take responsibility and to say they were sorry for their mistake.

Things settled down. And so we soldiered on. Family dinners now were only my dad, my mother-in-law and me. Steven came occasionally, but I could understand how it was difficult for him. These occasions, although pleasant, always served as yet another reminder of what was missing. It was easier not to have to face this reality. At two of these dinner get-togethers, Nana had a heart attack and emergency services had to be called on both occasions. I sent Nana off in the ambulance, took my dad back to the retirement home, then went to the hospital for long hours. After her second heart attack, by-pass surgery was in order, and this meant many months of recuperation. She stayed with me for several weeks, until she was able to manage on her own.

My dad also had a hospital stay. While in the retirement home, he coughed up some blood while I was there. I wish I had known that blood thinners were the cause. I may not have been so quick to get him to hospital, where his condition was bound to get worse. Having been healthy all his life, he wasn't used to hospitals and drugs. When I got him off the drugs, he became more himself. Yet again it was a very unpleasant experience, just two years after voicing my concerns in my report. Nothing had changed. When I asked the Hospital Ombudsperson, "What about the poor souls who don't have an advocate or family member to speak up for them?", her reply was stark. "They're poor souls!" she said.

Because of short staff, I arrived to find him restrained and alone in the hall. No one was in sight. I untied him and we walked the corridor, shaking in anger until the first nurse appeared. "How dare you tie up my Dad" I cried. I threatened to take my Dad out of there at that moment. This upset warranted a meeting with the floor manager, at which time I received an apology. She said it was against the law for patients to be restrained. The damage was done.

My anger, as a result of poor treatment was forever present, gnawing away in my mind. It would be seven years after my Mom's death that a hospital senior official was sitting directly in front of me at church. Was he sitting there for a reason? Was this God's way of giving me a message?..."Speak to him...find closure!" So, I tapped him on the shoulder and introduced myself. He phoned and left me a message the following week. He had gone through his files from all those years ago and found the correspondence. He now recalled and was apologetic for the poor treatment and indignities that were presented by the hospital staff. I asked him "How can anyone make excuses for rotting flesh? How can anyone answer a specialist's question when he asks "How long have her legs been like this?" – this doctor even added

"If she ever gets out of here!" I wish I could have made things better for my family while they were in hospital. It wasn't for lack of trying. Unfortunately for me and my family I told the hospital official his phone message was seven years too late. One doctor said "Our health system is not good for the doctors, it's not good for the nurses and it's not good for the patients." I have to agree with him. I hope, however, that some day I'll be able to let this anger go.

After his hospital stay, my dad could not return to the retirement home and instead went to a nursing home. The choices were far better in 2004, with at least three or four new nursing homes having been built locally, than in 2001 when I was presented with the possibility of finding a place for mom. However, the task still took a lot of time to research, organize and finalize. Unfortunately, my dad died in the nursing home in February of 2004, one month after moving in. He was 89. I thought it was unusual for a care worker to ask me if she could come in and see my Dad after he died. She wanted to have a look as she explained she had never seen a dead person. At the time it didn't bother me. Now that I think back, it seems odd.

Not another funeral! I couldn't face a crowd. This one had to be intimate because of his quiet and gentle nature, but always a jolly presence, as my Auntie Betty would say. A few of us sat in a circle; each of us remembering special moments as we lit four candles in his honour; one for our grief, one for courage to confront our sorrow and move forward, one for our memories, and one for the love we shared. We listened to a piece of music called, "No Farewells", written by our interim minister at the time. I still believe that my decision to have a small, intimate service for my dad was the right one. It was all I could cope with at the time and what he would have wanted. It pains me that some members of the family took offence at my decision. Years later, I still don't hear from some of them apparently because of this. Although I later wrote and apologized, wondering if, in hindsight I had made a mistake, I was told they were only taking my lead. A convenient excuse? They have their own busy lives.

The days ahead were grim, but soldier on we did. That was a common expression used in my Scottish background. Some days I don't know which was more difficult to do; to leave the house or to return to it after being away. Inside the walls of my home, I feel safe, but once I go outside the door, I become vulnerable and my wounds are uncovered. The reality of all the deaths makes me sick to my stomach. Yet I do my best to always offer people a cheery "hello", even when my heart is weighted with sorrow.

After my dad's death, I went to Scotland, my birthplace, for a visit. While there, I scattered my mom's and my dad's ashes in the Firth of Forth near Edinburgh. They would have liked that. I visited the homes of my grandparents and also where I lived as a child, before coming to Canada as a seven-year-old. I even found the grave of my parents' first baby, who died of meningitis in the early 1940's. My dad had come home to Scotland for the baby's arrival, such a happy time. Then he returned to Africa, where he was stationed at the time, only to be called back three weeks later after the baby's death. They never forgot her birthday and sometimes would say, "Ray would have been 49 today", or whatever age she would happen to be. After all those years, the memory was still strong. I must confess that only now do I appreciate the depth of their pain.

In December of 2004, my dad came to me in a dream. It seemed so real and I like to believe it was. He was standing in the doorway. I couldn't believe my eyes. I was awestruck, knowing that he had died. How could it possibly be him? He was younger, and very handsome, with hair. As he walked towards me, I hesitated to hug him, for fear of him not being real. Then I did hug him and told him, "I love you, Daddy." He said, "I love you too". I asked after Mommy. He replied, "I-V". At that moment, a nurse passed by us pushing a woman in a wheelchair. The woman had an I-V. She had silken white hair and as she turned to go up the ramp, I could see she was my mom. She didn't speak to me. She was so beautiful. I felt good about the visit. The dream was very comforting and I hope that on another occasion my mom will speak to me.

I wasn't with my mom or dad when they died, both early in the morning. I was there shortly after. In a way, I wish I could have been with them, but this was not meant to be. The anguish of my Mom's hospital stay had ended, and we were glad to leave after attending to details. It was nicer at the nursing home when I arrived. It was serene in my Dad's room; the nurse had left his music playing…

I'm No Awa Tae Bide Awa,
I'm no awa tae leave ye
I'm no awa tae bide awa
I'll ay come back an' see ye.

The words mean: I don't want to say good bye, I don't want to leave you, but I'll always come back and see you. This is one of our familiar and favourite Scottish tunes.

In many ways, this time of life signals a rebirth as we examine our individual past, as well as our familial past. As our parents' lives move toward completion, we are able to see what they did with their time on earth, what we have done so far with our time, and what we might want to do with the time we have left. These challenges and blessings are all part of the cycle of life.

*Picture taken on Thanksgiving Monday, four days
before my husband died on October 17, 1997.*

Happy Days

Reflections 10 Years On

It is difficult to know what to say to those friends who think that, after a certain period of time, I should be "getting over" it. They have not walked in my shoes and cannot know how difficult this journey has been and continues to be for me. I would not wish it on any of them. I doubt I will ever "get over" losing Bill or Richard or any of my loved ones. Instead, time has allowed me to learn coping skills; to keep their memory alive by doing constructive "grief work" so that I will be forever connected to them in my heart.

I still have struggles, and tears over my loved ones still fall. I know how my friend feels when she says she goes to bed at night with a big lump in her throat. She lost her husband to breast cancer. She says her tears wet her pillow and she wakes up with a gray cloud over her head, missing him to share her day with. I know and understand how she feels. We have our self talks, reminding ourselves how lucky we are in so many ways. Even though we realize that, it doesn't take away the pain. It makes our hearts break that our loved ones are not with us physically. To come home and not have anyone to share all the ordinary things that go on in life, never mind the challenges that we face, to have no one to balance anxieties and share joys is hell on earth. We read the right books; we do yoga, pray, and even smile when we're sad. We still feel like empty shells, pretending to the world. Sometimes our "now" feels very empty.

Every year at church, we have a remembrance service at which the names of loved ones who have passed into the mystery of death are read aloud. The service is called Communion of Saints; we remember that God is the one who is the author of life, of death, of life beyond death. Together, we remember the communion of people who have gone before us. For a couple of weeks prior to this service, we have the opportunity to write the names in a book and that year, 2007, 140 names had been entered. If people are coming forward with 140 names of people they love who have died, that is a clear message that we need to recognize such loss, especially in a culture that pushes away death and grief. To hear the names of loved ones spoken aloud, with the sound of a flute in the background, can be a very emotional experience. A friend asked me, "Why do they do it?" I was quick to say, "To remember!" but she couldn't understand why we would make ourselves vulnerable, and want to invite the return of sadness and tears. For me, remembering Bill and Richard and the other members of my family who have died makes me feel more alive and connected to them. Death leaves a heartache no one can heal; love leaves a memory no one can steal. I recognize now that my task is to try to let go of needing to understand why others don't feel the same as I do. The journey of grief is different for everyone. What helps one person may not serve another.

The fact remains that no one is exempt from the twists and turns of fate, which may, at any time, take the possessions, situations, and people we love away from us. Ironically, it is sometimes this kind of loss that awakens us to thankfulness and understanding that goes deeper than being superficially grateful when things go our way. Illness and near-miss accidents can wake us up to the deeper realization that we are truly lucky to be alive!

This journey through grief takes real work and often courage. I could have easily wallowed in my sorrow, but that is not meant for me. I have benefited from grief counselling and have spent countless hours making creative memory books. The phenomenon of creative memory books was created in 1987 by a woman in the U.S. who gave small workshops at the insistence of her friends. The popularity of making the books has skyrocketed and has become a fun way to preserve the past, enrich the present and inspire hope for the future. The books are put together using acid-free water and lignin-free bindings. Lignin in the pulp is what makes paper go brown as it ages. Because this has been removed, the photos and creative artwork done on each page are preserved for a lifetime.

I've made two creative memory books. One has pictures of great grandparents, grandparents, Bill, me, Steven, Richard and Kipper. Because Richard was seven years younger than Steven, many of the pictures on one page show him looking up at his older brother. I called this "Adoration". The last page reads:

Hold onto what is good –
Even if it is a handful of earth
Hold onto what you believe –
Even if it is a tree which stands by itself
Hold onto what you must do –
Even if it is a long way from here
Hold onto life –
Even when it is easier letting go
Hold onto my hand –
Even when I have gone away from you.

This is one of the most beautiful pieces of poetry I have ever read. I heard it first at Papa's funeral, who was the grandfather of my friends, Linda and Laurie.

The second memory book contains memorabilia after the deaths, i.e. Bill's eulogy, given by our good friend Rick, the newspaper clippings after Richard's death, the article written by his hockey coach, pictures of the memorial presentations, the cemetery and commemorative plaques in the garden. It also holds pictures of the tattoos on the boys' arms.

So far, Steven has not been able to look at these books because they push him into a deeper state of sadness. Perhaps some day, they will give him some comfort. That is my wish and hope. When he gives himself permission to sort through the range of emotions that are present, he will in turn create space for himself to begin the healing process. Once we consciously acknowledge that our "unwelcome" emotions are present, we are more able to soothe our sorrow. In so doing, we become more open to our natural ability to heal ourselves.

Grieving is not a process that keeps us rooted in our thoughts of fear and sadness. For the moment we might feel despondent but, by expressing and coping with our true feelings, we face our sadness head-on. When we allow ourselves to accept and deal fully with our loss, we are then able to continue our life's journey with a much more positive and accepting outlook. This makes it easier for us to see that our grief is ephemeral. We come to understand that, just like our moments of happiness, it too will pass.

In addition to the two creative memory books, I have also designed a garden at the cemetery and worked there many hours surrounded by my loved ones. The serenity and quietness of the location brings me comfort. The plaque says, "If tears could build a stairway, and memories a lane, I'd walk right up to Heaven and bring you home again." A few of my friends were a big help to me while I was planning the memorial garden. As always, friends plant seeds of hope, pull out weeds of despair and harvest real joy.

Our Vancouver friends, Peter and Helen, placed a plaque on the wall of their deck, overlooking Howe Sound, where we spent many happy occasions. The plaque says:

"Bill Stronach 1946 – 1997 A good friend who left us too soon. To Bill, the glass was always half full. We will miss his sense of humour."

Occasionally I take the notion to browse through memorabilia and read some of the heart-warming letters and keepsakes. Our dentist wrote after Bill's death:

"He seemed to take life around him in stride, always in a very affable manner, and yes, with that smile…a good solid husband and father."

He wrote again after Richard's death:

"Richard was the quiet, unassuming lanky defence star, the key to a team's success." The strength of the love he and Bill shared with me will get me by this time of despair. "Some people never come to know such a strong family love", he said.

On the occasion of having new carpet laid, my mother-in-law asked the installers if they would also lay an accent rug in her bedroom. For one of the men, this might be too big a job, but he would see at the end of the day. The other young man had recognized a picture hanging on the wall and connected that with our last name. It was a family portrait with our dog, so he immediately made the connection. He confided that his younger brother had been a friend and teammate of Richard's and recalled the day he came home from the funeral ten years ago feeling so distraught. Again, things like this serve to assure us that Richard lives on in the hearts of those who knew and loved him. He offered to come back with his younger brother and do this job for my mother-in-law in Richard's memory. Like clockwork, they arrived the next evening, and it was nice to reconnect with Andriy, whom I hadn't seen since before Richard's death. This was a very touching gesture and their kindness was appreciated by both Muriel and me.

The bench at the cemetery, being exposed to the elements after many years, was looking in need of a little restoration; i.e. varnishing. My mother-in-law, Muriel suggested we get up there and attend to this chore. A short time after this realization, and before we did anything, we were surprised to see that someone had taken care of this for us. A shiny new bench and I didn't have to do the work. I sent a note of appreciation to the Supervisor of Cemetery Services. She explained that the restoration of my family's bench was part of an overall bench refurbishment programme that was completed in 2008. They were happy to hear that we were most pleased. Sometimes the timing is remarkable, as if our prayers are being answered. Or, as my Auntie Nette would say, "Everything's tinged with mercy."

I see the months and the years passing. Most are full of associations that stir up old memories. My dad's birthday is in January, his death in February, as well as my father-in-law's birthday and my mom & dad's wedding anniversary on Valentines Day. March is the month of my son's birthday and his death, Kipper's death, an uncle's death and the memorial presentation. April is when my father-in-law and an aunt died. May 30th, 1970, was when Bill and I were married. We also remember the wedding anniversary of my in-laws on the 5th of June, the day before Steven's birthday. My birthday is also in June. Celebrations just aren't the same. It was in the warm summer month of July that my mom went into hospital. She died there in September, nine days after her 84th birthday. My husband died in October, a few days before his birthday. Add to that the holiday occasions, and it seems a lot to cope with. The reminders are always a constant. However, the anticipation is always worse than the actual event. And of course, once it passes, there is relief to have survived yet another challenge and/or month.

Although I haven't seen an old school friend for over forty five years, we have kept in touch by correspondence. She lives in Montreal and has a private practice as a psychotherapist. We were the best of elementary school friends as well as high school. Now we keep in touch by e-mail. I said in a recent message to her that I could hardly believe it myself that I've written a book, but that "of course, it's good grief work to get it down on paper and out of the damn in my chest." She replied:

"As a therapist, couldn't help but remark on interesting spelling slip (damn). Sometimes a typo is just a typo, but it could be worth thinking about any anger you have been carrying in your chest. You have every right to be damn angry – it's just

not to get stuck there – and I understand that your chest and heart must be so full it could feel dammed up. Just thought you might want to be aware of a message from yourself to yourself and to check on any level of resentment (anger) you still harbour, as it can be toxic for you. Figured since you are writing a book on grief, you would be interested in what your unconscious may be revealing to you."

I'm quite sure this was just a typo, but I thought very observant of her, and something that only a person with a knowledge of the grieving process would pick up on.

When I look back at the last ten years, I am often amazed to see how I have survived so many trials and surmounted obstacles. There's a saying that God doesn't give us any more than we can handle. To me, thinking that we do not have the strength to handle what is before us can be likened to the hard surface of a frozen lake. The surface appears to be an impenetrable fact, but when we break through it, we find a deep well of energy and inspiration trapped beneath the icy barrier. Each time we break through, we reach a new understanding of the strength we hold within ourselves. I believe that, with work, we can get to the other side of our grief or at least close to it. With strength and grace, I will survive and discover the richest possible meaning to my new life. A grief victim struggles to maintain a state of normalcy. A survivor knows normal no longer exists.

There is a fundamental worth, sacredness and beauty to each human person. The basic challenge of life is to feel, honour, and cherish that worth in ourselves and in others, especially in the face of the hurts, wounds and betrayals of life. I have discovered this worth through music, friendships and community outreach. Fully experiencing our own hurt is the gateway to compassion toward other human beings. Friendships are to be cherished, and I am blessed in having strong bonds with so many wonderful people, who are there for me when the chips are down. A survivor wants someone to share their journey. A grief victim wants someone to cure their grief.

Truly, it takes great courage to sit with our feelings, to surrender ourselves to their powerful energies, especially those that rock us and knock us. No-one wants to feel hurt, or lonely, or afraid. So all too often we strive to push our feelings aside, trying to avoid anxiety, vulnerability and depression, all the while telling ourselves we will deal with them later. If we don't deal with them, we end up storing them in our hearts, minds and bodies. This is when stress and other health issues can arise. Sometimes it may appear easier to distract ourselves, to take our minds off our sadness. Yet in my experience, this only makes healing more difficult because when we refuse to listen to where we are "in the moment", the emotions we refuse to experience only grow in intensity. They will always return to manifest themselves in more powerful and less comfortable ways. Denying what our bodies feel, and want to feel, can lead to trouble now or down the line. This is why staying in the thick of our feelings, no matter how scary at times, is the best thing we can do for ourselves.

After so much grief in my own life, and in the lives of people I love, I wholeheartedly believe that the best way to overcome grief is by living through it with courage and steadfast prayer.

We all have a purpose in this life with lessons to learn. Over the last ten years, this has been unfolding for me and has formed who I was, who I am, and who I am becoming.

There is always room for growth and learning. I took a course in pastoral care which allowed me to learn that my journey in reaching out to others is widespread. This training in ministry has given me some comfort as I've learned to pray, to give thanks first, and then to ask our Heavenly Father for help and support. I enjoyed the warmth of the teaching team and look forward to sharing their knowledge and teachings with others, and to also be a comfort to the suffering.

I am also now able to offer my listening expertise on a volunteer basis at a Distress Centre. For this too, it was necessary to complete a course.

I am also very mindful of my mother-in-law's reassuring words. She says "I read your horoscope every morning Enid and the sum total is "hang in there. You are strong and can cope with it all." I will continue to do my best, as I live by the three "E's", Energy, Enthusiasm and Empathy, and the three "F's", Faith, Family and Friends.

And again, I recall the story about new life, as that of the butterfly. I believe the same for my loved ones, who have only left our physical world. With this in mind, I must "Soldier On."

Epilogue

Upon completion of 'Soldier On', I have had many readers ask "How is Steven doing?" And so I add these words to complete my story.

In times of trouble, we develop behaviours that allow us to get past challenges with the least amount of pain. These behaviours provided survival for Steven both mentally and physically in the years following all of our losses. However, these defence mechanisms weren't always healthy choices.

Without any grand announcement or sudden shift, Muriel and I became aware that change was happening, as if by grace perhaps. We never gave up hope and always maintained an optimistic attitude along with infinite patience.

Time, effort and maturity have allowed a subtle and comfortable change for Steven with the result that he is now in his own home and taking responsibility for all that goes with it. He has also taken the necessary steps to once again have a driver's license.

As Steven's own healing has evolved, his natural compassion and his willingness to help others has taught him many lessons. It is said that adversity builds character....our spiritual ABC's so to speak. As time passes, it is what we do with that time that gives us the ability to rise above the old habits and patterns to discover the new truths that lie before us.

In the garden of our lives, tilling and nurturing the soil continues. The laws of nature that govern the growth of plants also oversee our maturation and changes. Life continues to unfold, but the pendulum seems to have settled comfortably in the center, restoring balance for us all.

Steven and Enid 2011

90 Years Young!

"Muriel Stronach"...Her 90th Birthday Party Invitation...November 2009.

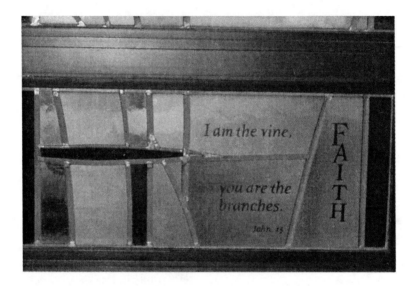

This window, in the Narthex of Glen Abbey United church is dedicated by Enid Stronach with the faith that enables us to "Soldier On" through the journey of life.

*I went to visit Enid the morning I received the news about
her 16 yr. old son, Richard, who had died on the ice at his
hockey game the night before. This was just a mere five
months after Bill had died and I couldn't possibly imagine
how Enid could survive this next turn of events. I will never
forget the sounds I heard when I arrived at Enid's. It was,
purely and simply, a "mother's heartbreaking lament", a
haunting, wailing cry that came from her soul and it touched
me down to my depths. How in God's name could this
woman ever go on??? I can hear those sounds to this day,
some 12 years later. It was life altering for me as her friend.
All the more reason to know that "hope" lives inside all of
us, even the most broken. Enid is a true testament to this and
I find myself referring to her during my own personal
hardships, having learned through her that life is never
hopeless and that within us all and with time, healing is
possible and life can be lived again.*

Debbie Findlay